Mark Twain

Blackwell Introductions to Literature

This series sets out to provide concise and stimulating introductions to literary subjects. It offers books on major authors (from John Milton to James Joyce), as well as key periods and movements (from Anglo-Saxon literature to the contemporary). Coverage is also afforded to such specific topics as "Arthurian Romance". While some of the volumes are classed as "short" introductions (under 200 pages), others are slightly longer books (around 250 pages). All are written by outstanding scholars as texts to inspire newcomers and others: non-specialists wishing to revisit a topic, or general readers. The prospective overall aim is to ground and prepare students and readers of whatever kind in their pursuit of wider reading.

Mark Twain

A Short Introduction

Stephen Railton

Blackwell Publishing

350 Main Street, Malden, MA 02148–5020, USA
108 Cowley Road, Oxford OX4 1JF, UK
550 Swanston Street, Carlton, Victoria 3053, Australia

First published 2004 by Blackwell Publishing Ltd

Library of Congress Cataloging-in-Publication Data

Railton, Stephen, 1948–
Mark Twain, a short introduction / Stephen Railton.
p. cm. – (Blackwell introductions to literature)
Includes index.
ISBN 0–631–23473–X (hardcover: alk. paper) –
ISBN 0–631–23474–8
(pbk.: alk. paper)
1. Twain, Mark, 1835–1910—Criticism and
interpretation.   2. Humorous
stores, American—History and criticism.   I. Title.   II. Series.

PS1338.R35   2003
818'.409—dc21
2003004957

A catalogue record for this title is available from the
British Library.

Set in 10/13pt Meridian
by Graphicraft Ltd, Hong Kong
Printed and bound in the United Kingdom
by T.J. International, Padstow, Cornwall

For further information on
Blackwell Publishing, visit our website:
http://www.blackwellpublishing.com

To the memory of my mother, Marjorie Elizabeth Marks Railton, whose childhood was spent alongside the river in LaGrange, Missouri

Contents

Figures

All images courtesy the Clifton Waller Barrett Library, Department of Special Collections, University of Virginia.

Preface

Keeping an introduction to Mark Twain short means having to make a lot of tough choices. I've chosen to emphasize his ambitions and achievements as a writer: each of the following six chapters is focused on one of his major works, from *Innocents Abroad* to *Pudd'nhead Wilson*. While looking closely at these texts, though, I also try to locate them in the contexts defined by Samuel Clemens' life, his career as Mark Twain, and the larger American environment of his times. Two of the questions I keep coming back to are: what did Twain's books mean to his contemporaries? And what did being "Mark Twain" mean to Sam Clemens? By trying to answer them, however briefly and partially, we can explore what the United States has been as a nation and what each of us is trying to be as a person. Twain's words made it easier for Americans in his day to move toward their future as a world power; they still confront us with the challenge of the nation's history as a democratic work in progress. And as the country's first great literary celebrity, he can illuminate a great deal about the ways in which we become somebody by performing our selves for others.

Be good & you will be lonesome.

Mark Twain

Frontispiece photograph for *Following the Equator* (Hartford: American Publishing Company, 1897)

1

Going East
Innocents Abroad

In June, 1867, Samuel Clemens was 31 years old, and the United States was 90. After years of uncertainty and struggle, the future was looking bright for both of them. America had come through the war between North and South that threatened its existence as a nation. It was finishing the railroad that would span the continent from east to west. It probably was already beginning to feel the summons to the central place on the international stage that it would claim by the end of the century.

America's rise to its role as world power occurred during the same years as Clemens' rise to the status of world celebrity. Clemens' struggle toward that place dated back to his childhood. The family he had been born into, like many on the country's southwestern frontier, was always rich in social pretensions and chronically strapped for cash. Before his death in 1847, John Clemens, Sam's father, store-keeper, sometime lawyer, land speculator, kept restlessly searching for success, which explains why in 1839, four years after Sam had been born in a cabin in Florida, Missouri, the family moved to the economically more promising river town of Hannibal. Unlike Tom Sawyer, however, John Clemens found no treasure in the village. When he died, Sam was 12; the loss forced him to work to help his mother make ends meet. He stayed in school long enough to complete nine years of education in a series of one-room schoolhouses, but by the time he was 15 he was working fulltime. For the next 15 years his employment history suggests he inherited both his father's restlessness and his economic bad luck. Sam's first association with words and writing came through a series of jobs in printing offices, first in Hannibal, then in St Louis; at seventeen he ran off to see the World's Fair in New York, and worked in print shops there and in Philadelphia for about half a year before coming back to the Mississippi. In 1857 he apprenticed himself to Horace Bixby to become a riverboat pilot, gaining his license two years later. Piloting was a well-paying, prestigious job, but in 1861 the Civil War halted commerce on the river. After two weeks in an irregular Confederate militia unit, Sam ran off again: he lit out for the Territory of Nevada in company with his brother Orion, who had just been appointed territorial secretary. Safe from the War, he vowed to himself not to go home again until he had made a fortune. There were fortunes to be made on this frontier – in timber, in silver, in mining speculations – but Sam found no treasure either.

Intermittently during these years he had written and published a number of short pieces in various newspapers. In keeping with the journalistic conventions of the day, he signed these pieces with pseudonyms, including "W. Epaminondas Adrastus Perkins" and "Thomas Jefferson Snodgrass." While looking for precious metals in the deserts of Nevada, he submitted several letters to the Virginia City (Nevada) *Territorial Enterprise* under the pen name "Josh," and their popularity resulted in the offer of a position on the paper. With no prospects as a prospector, Clemens became a professional writer in September, 1862. As a frontier newspaperman, he wrote mostly news stories, though he first began to acquire a name for himself with some hoaxes published as news. In February, 1863, that name became "Mark Twain," when for reasons that remain unknown he decided to sign three political reports from the territorial capital of Carson City with those two words.

"Mark Twain" was no overnight sensation, and the next several years display the same pattern of restlessness. By 1864 he was working as a reporter in San Francisco, and in 1866 became a traveling correspondent for two different California papers, traveling first westward to Hawaii (then called the Sandwich Islands) and next eastward, to New York. But he had found his calling: as he put it in a letter to Orion in the fall of 1865: "I *have* had a 'call' to literature, of a low order – *i.e.* humorous."[1] His ambivalence about (to quote another phrase from that letter) "seriously scribbling to excite the laughter of God's creatures" was real – "Poor, pitiful business!" is how the letter winds up – and would persist throughout his career. But by the time

"Mark Twain" was three years old – by June, 1867 – that persona had already brought Clemens two different kinds of national recognition. His humorous sketch, "Jim Smiley and His Jumping Frog," had leaped from the pages of New York's *Saturday Press* (where it first appeared in November, 1865) and into newspapers across the country, where it made a big splash with the American reading public. And less than a year later he proved he could excite their laughter by talking as well as scribbling when he revised his Hawaiian correspondence into a humorous lecture called "Our Fellow Savages of the Sandwich Islands"; he performed it first in San Francisco, then toured with it through a dozen Pacific slope mining towns, gave it again in St Louis and elsewhere when he revisited the Mississippi in early 1867, and then delighted two different audiences in New York City with it. At the end of April he even brought out a book: *The Celebrated Jumping Frog of Calaveras County, and Other Sketches*. It was not just the frog who was becoming a celebrity.

In June, 1867, Mark Twain (to use the name by which the country was beginning to know him) and America were ready to take on the world. At least, that is one way to understand the cruise of the *Quaker City*, the six-month trip to Europe and the Holy Land (as the Middle East was then called) that became the basis for the book with which Twain's literary career was really launched. The trip itself was a first: by chartering a sea-going side-wheel steamship to take them to the Old World, the 60 *Quaker City* passengers became America's first organized tour group. As American tourists heading east, however, they sailed on what Twain refers to as "the tide of a great popular movement."[2] As Henry James' tales of such "innocents abroad" as Daisy Miller affronting her destiny in Europe suggest, during the last third of the 19th century more and more Americans made pilgrimages to the cultural shrines of London, Paris, Rome and the other stops on the Grand Tour. Many went still further east, to Palestine, to visit the sites made sacred by their Biblical associations. Conceived by the fashionable Plymouth Church in Brooklyn, the *Quaker City* expedition advertised itself as an "Excursion to the Holy Land," but on the way there were arranged stops at "Intermediate Points of Interest" across the Mediterranean, with plenty of time provided for junkets to places like Paris, where another World's Fair was in progress.

People for whom the words "Mark Twain" conjure up the image of a poor white boy and an enslaved black man floating down a river on a raft might have a hard time locating him on the *Quaker City* trip. Most of his fellow passengers were eminently respectable, genteel, devout and well-to-do. Samuel Clemens, for example, could not have afforded the trip: the $1,250 cost of his passage and his expenses on land were paid by the *Alta California*, a San Franciso paper. But Clemens was a very ambitious man. He accepted without any conscious misgiving the advice he was given in the Sandwich Islands by diplomat Anson Burlingame: "Never affiliate with inferiors; always *climb*."[3] The *Quaker City* trip gave him a chance to take two steps upward. He apprenticed himself to another passenger, a slightly older woman named Mary Fairbanks, wife of a wealthy Cleveland publisher. For the next several years, until his career was established, he called her "Mother" and referred to himself as her "Cub," and from her took lessons in navigating the tastes and proprieties of the middle class audience he knew he wanted to reach. And through his roommate on the cruise, a young man named Charley Langdon, the son of a rich coal dealer in Elmira, New York, he would meet the woman he married, Charley's sister Olivia. With that marriage the child from a cabin in the southwest would find entrance into the mansions of the east, where he spent the rest of his life.

The almost sixty reports he wrote for the *Alta* and several New York papers also attracted the attention of the publishing world. One publisher in particular, Elisha Bliss, head of the American Publishing Company in Hartford, was particularly attracted by one letter, the irascible "valedictory" to the trip Twain printed in the New York *Herald* the day after the *Quaker City* docked. There Twain calls the pilgrimage "a funeral excursion without a corpse" (644), and said that life with his fellow-passengers, whom he calls the "saints," consisted of "solemnity, decorum, dinner, dominoes, devotions, slander" (645). Some of those passengers publically took offense at Twain's satirical account, and in the controversy thus stirred up Bliss saw publicity, popularity and profits. His company published books "by subscription," which meant that customers bought them from door-to-door sales agents. Thick, well-illustrated travel books were a staple of the subscription book trade, but until Bliss wrote Twain to ask if he was interested in making a book out of his *Quaker City* experience, no one had tried selling a humorous text this way. Twain wrote back to ask "what amount of money" such a venture might earn, adding that that question "has a degree of importance for me which is almost beyond my own comprehension."[4] There would be a lot of money for them both, Bliss assured him – and on that basis at the end of 1867 Twain committed himself to writing a book.

Published in 1869 as *The Innocents Abroad, or The New Pilgrims' Progress*, the book was very successful. In its first year it sold 70,000 copies, and throughout Twain's lifetime it remained the single best-selling of all his books. It established many of the patterns that recur throughout his career. All of his major books, for example, were published "by subscription," even after Twain left Bliss to set up his own publishing firm. Four more of them were literally travel books: *Roughing It* (1872), *A Tramp Abroad* (1880), *Life on the Mississippi* (1883), *Following the Equator* (1897). Traveling is an important motif in many of the others: the river trip in *Adventures of Huckleberry Finn* (1885), travel in time as well as space in *A Connecticut Yankee in King Arthur's Court* (1889), even the balloon voyage in *Tom Sawyer, Abroad* (1894). As the first act in Mark Twain's performance as a beloved popular author and entertainer, *Innocents Abroad* is the text with which an introduction to him should start. It is also a good place to begin appreciating his art as a humorist and his project as a realist.

The book followed the well-established formula for successful subscription publication. It was long, 651 pages long: subscription customers were often people who never went into bookstores, and who bought only a few books in a year; "the rural-district reader likes to see that he has got his money's worth," as a reviewer in *The Nation* put it, "and no man ever saw a book-agent with a small volume in his hand."[5] Subscription buyers also liked pictures: Bliss' edition of *Innocents Abroad* contained, as it proclaims on the titlepage, "two hundred and thirty-four illustrations." Like many passages in Twain's text, many of the illustrations are serious, even solemn. His account is often saturated with facts (the cathedral in Milan is "five hundred feet long by one hundred and eighty wide" and has "7,148 marble statues" [180]), and his prose often self-consciously eloquent (the eyes of the Sphinx "look steadfastly back upon the things they knew before History was born – before Tradition had being," and so on [629]), and the corresponding full-page illustrations of Cathedral and Sphinx are suitable for framing. Subscription customers who could only fantasize about being able to afford the Grand Tour expected travel books to provide in their words and pictures a vicarious chance to see the world. But the great virtue of *Innocents Abroad*, the feature that Bliss emphasized in his advertising campaign, was the chance it gave readers to laugh at what they saw. As a narrative it goes to the same Old World sites as dozens of travelogues published in the decade after the Civil War, but what made it a hit was that its first-person narrator provides so much fun as a character and a guide.

In the book's protagonist American readers got their first full glimpse of "Mark Twain." He is the most innocent of the innocents abroad. If the typical travel book author sets himself up as an authority, "Mark Twain" is defined by his inexperience. This is the aesthetic or structural basis of his readers' pleasure: the way the book's "I" allows them to look down on his misadventures as a tenderfoot or naif. What Henry James' American pilgrims from Daisy to Christopher Newman to Isabel Archer don't know can have tragic consequences, but what happens to "Mark Twain" in the Old World is funny, and the comedy provides the reader with a superior position from which to enjoy the fate of innocence. The encounter with a Parisian barber is typical of the shtick. The narrator's naive expectations set up the joke: "from earliest infancy it had been a cherished ambition of mine to be shaved some day in a palatial barbershop in Paris" (113). The snapper is sprung a couple hundred words later when dream gives way to flesh-and-blood reality: the French barber "swooped down upon me like the genius of destruction. The first rake of his razor loosened the very hide from my face and lifted me out of the chair. I stormed and raved, and the other boys enjoyed it." The comedy here is very carefully stage managed: in the explicit laughter of "the other boys" – two traveling companions – readers are given all the permission they could want to enjoy the "I's" discomfiture. Similar scenes occur regularly throughout the book. Being shaved again by a barber in Venice, buying kid gloves from a pretty Spanish girl in Gibraltar, trying out the supposed delights of a Turkish bath in Constantinople – the narrative repeatedly makes its central character appear ridiculous. It is a pure pose, of course, as deliberately fashioned a comic persona as Charlie Chaplin's "Little Tramp." It is also, as Twain learned early in his career as a humorist, a very effective means to ingratiate himself with audiences expecting something to laugh at: publically, at least, he was always willing to let them laugh at him.

Naivete is a primary source of Twain's humor. Readers of the "Jumping Frog" are privileged to laugh at the ignorance of nearly everyone in the sketch: at Smiley, for the trick that the mysterious stranger plays on him; at Simon Wheeler, for the deadpan seriousness with which he narrates the doings of dogs with names like "Andrew Jackson" and a frog named "Daniel Webster"; and at "Mark Twain," who frames the tale as the aggrieved victim of a hoax that forces him to suffer through Wheeler's interminable ramblings. Twain was a rhetorical opportunist, always looking for the best way to exploit the comic potenial of a subject and so keep readers entertained. The "Mark Twain" he develops for the "Jumping Frog" is a fussy easterner, appalled rather than amused by the antics and idiom of the roughs in a mining camp – someone who would feel at home among the "saints" on the *Quaker City*. *Innocents Abroad* (including the scores of illustrations that feature images of him) casts him in a different role: rougher, more western. He gives few details about his background, but does brag about taking a glorious ride on the overland stage coach, building a Humbolt house in the Nevada deserts and being well acquainted with the beauty of Lake Tahoe. The promotional poster that Bliss designed to help his agents sell the book capitalizes on this western, unmistakably "new world" aspect of the narrator's identity: on it the author appears as a kind of bourgeois savage, complete with tomahawk, bow and arrow, advancing with suspicious hostility on the Old World (see Figure 1). American readers are certainly invited to laugh at this caricature, but they are also encouraged to identify with it: on the carpet bag are two sets of initials – "M.T." and "U.S."

Hank Morgan begins his time-traveling account of King Arthur's court by saying "I am an American . . . a Yankee of the Yankees." The narrator of *Innocents Abroad* is not this explicit, but his American readers knew on every page that "M.T." was one of "US." Another target of his humor is the expatriate, the type of American who adopts European airs: people like "Lloyd B. Williams," who signs the register of an Italian hotel as with "*et trois amis, ville de* Boston," or Mr. Gordon, who does not recognize his name anymore, except as "M'sieu Gor-r-*dong*" (233–4). For his part, the narrator holds firmly to his American identity. "The boys" (as he calls himself and the two fellow Americans he usually travels with) rename the villages in the Middle East to make them easier to spell and pronounce: *Temnin-el-Foka*, for example, becomes "Jacksonville" (438). Like Robinson Crusoe, who immediately establishes his superiority to the native he saves by telling him his name is "Friday," beginning in Paris "the boys" decide to call all

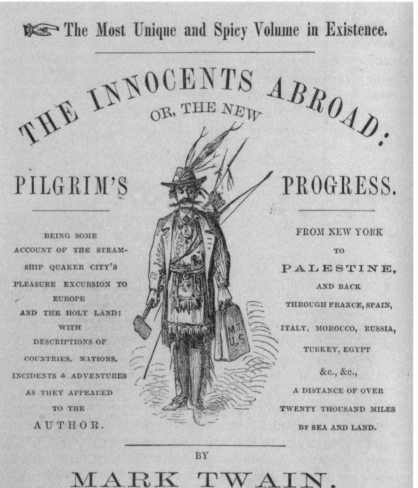

FIGURE 1   Poster from the sales prospectus for *The Innocents Abroad*
(Hartford: American Publishing Company, 1869)

their hired guides "Ferguson" (120). Guide-baiting quickly becomes one of their chief sources of pleasure. While a guide points out all the historical, artistic or high cultural sights, they pretend indifference or even scorn. With one phrase in particular they find a fool-proof way to defend themselves against everything that the Old World has to offer, and also shatter each Ferguson's smugness – "Is he dead?" Whether they are supposed to be admiring a painting by Michaelangelo or an Egyptian mummy, repeatedly asking the "Is he dead?" is guaranteed to amuse them and distress the guide.

Twain seems serious about the moral he provides at the journey's end: "Travel is fatal to prejudice, bigotry and narrow-mindedness, and many of our people need it sorely on these accounts" (650). As a sentiment, that is safely conventional. As a way to sum up the narrative, however, it is very misleading. The prejudices that *Innocents Abroad* most effectively subverts are not those that Americans, "our people," might have *against* the Old World, but rather the preconceptions they probably have *in its favor*. The presumption on which the Grand Tour was founded was the idea that only by going to Europe could an American acquire real "culture," a belief rooted in the country's neo-colonial inferiority complex. From James Fenimore Cooper onward many American writers complained that the nation had "listened too long to the courtly muses of Europe." That was how Ralph Waldo Emerson put it in 1837 in his "American Scholar" oration, where he added: "The spirit of the American freeman is already suspected to be timid, imitative, tame." There is a kind of pun in the way Twain treats the "Old Masters": his irreverence can liberate the enslaved minds of his readers. "I never felt so fervently thankful, so soothed, so tranquil, so filled with a blessed peace as I did yesterday when I learned that Michaelangelo was dead" (288). Even their laughter is liberating. In those scenes of his discomfiture, for instance, he is not the only one made to look ridiculous. The difference between what he expected from a Parisian barbershop and the reality exposes not just his innocence, but also the shabbiness of the Old World. As the narrative repeatedly depicts it, the Old World is the opposite of naive – it is, well, old. Adjectives like "dirty," "impoverished," "decrepit," "ruined," "decayed," and so on are deployed again and again. "Is it dead?" Maybe not, but it is clearly dying. Is "The Last Supper" really the greatest painting in the world? Maybe it was, "once. But it was three hundred years ago"; now it is "dimmed with age," "scaled and marred" (191–3).

In his Preface, Twain promises to show his American reader "Europe and the East" exactly as "*he*" would see them "if he looked at them with his own eyes instead of the eyes of those who traveled in those countries before him" (vi). Most contemporary travel writers, including Henry James in his international tales, exasperated the anxieties Americans already felt toward the Old World from which so much of their culture was derived. In the first scene of James' novel *The American*, for example, the paintings in the Louvre inspire the title character "for the first time in his life, with a vague self-mistrust." Travel books typically capitalize on such self-doubts by placing their expertise at the service of the sight-seer's ignorance. Twain's calculated naivete has just the opposite effect: rather than implying there is so much Americans need to learn from the museums and cathedrals of Europe, *Innocents Abroad* suggests that there is little of value Americans don't already know; instead of submitting themselves humbly to the Old World as a kind of post-graduate education, they are given that world to enjoy as a diversion.

Rather than kneel before the cultural shrines he visits, Twain's iconoclastic persona prefers to rock the pedestals on which the idols sit; their fall from greatness is an occasion for comedy, not tragedy; the high ground, culturally and aesthetically, is bestowed on the American reader who is privileged to look down on the process. If Europe had a great past, it's clear that both the present and the future belong to the newer world.

American readers had good reasons for *wanting* to see the Old World this way – laughing at Europe helped them transform their national self-image from former colonial dependent to potential imperial power – but whether they *could* see the world with their own eyes is a question that the book takes seriously. Not too seriously, of course: Twain's main purpose throughout is to keep his audience entertained. But at points the text betrays a different ambition: to enlighten its readers, by working to show them what they *should* see. One such point occurs in front of "The Last Supper," as Twain listens to the other tourists "apostrophizing wonders and beauties . . . which had faded out of the picture and gone, a hundred years before they were born" (192). "How," he wonders, "can they see what is not visible?" That is a question he knows the answer to. Essentially this same scene is enacted again in the Holy Land, at a landmark called "The Fountain of the Virgin," where the object of attention is a young

Nazarene girl. To Twain's eyes she is pleasant enough, but short and homely; one by one, however, the other members of his party pronounce her "tall," and remark the "Madonna-like beauty of her countenance." What they "see" is not visible either. Instead, they take it directly from one of the guide books to the Holy Land they use as "authorities," and from which their ideas of reality are derived (531).

Books as pre-texts, as occasions for his own texts, play a crucial role in Twain's career. One of his basic tactics as a comic writer, for example, was to start with a well-known work or genre and write a burlesque or parody of it: his send up of didactic Sunday School tales, "The Story of the Bad Little Boy That Bore a Charmed Life," published in the same year as "The Jumping Frog," is an early example of this technique. *Innocents Abroad* contains two such burlesque tales within its narrative: an anti-sentimental account of Heloise and Abelard (chapter 15) and a slangy pseudo-Arabian Nights romance about the Seven Sleepers – Johannes, Trumps, Gift, High, Low, Jack and The Game (chapter 41). As a humorist, then, Mark Twain often practices the art of *re*-writing other books. Behind that, however, were his goals as a realist; for him, that project can be summed up as the art of *un*-writing other books. Like the other American realists of his generation, including his friend and sometime editor William Dean Howells, Twain's writing explores the way people's understanding of reality is often pre-determined by the books they read: their interpretations of the world are based not on their own experience, but instead on what the textual authorities tell them is "there." That conditioning is actually the source of his protagonist's misadventures with barbers and Turkish baths: he is not strictly speaking naive, but badly misinformed by the romantic stories he has read naively, believing their fictions. Late in the trip he acknowledges this in one of the book's most significant phrases: "I can see easily enough that if I wish to profit by this tour and come to a correct understanding of the matters of interest connected with it, I must studiously and faithfully unlearn a great many things I have somehow absorbed" (486). Many of the best moments in his books are scenes of "unlearning."

Thus *Innocents Abroad* is both a travel book and an anti-travel book. Just as Tom Sawyer will tell Huck that they must do exactly what the books say when they dig for treasure or organize a robber gang, the *Quaker City* tourists carry a lot of texts wherever they go: "were we not traveling by the guide-book?" (435) Just as Huck's illiteracy, however, offers a kind of antidote to Tom's fatuous reliance on his "authorities," Mark Twain's narrative defines itself against the accounts of previous authors. One place where the act of un-writing becomes overt is at the Sea of Galilee. After describing the scenery himself as "expressionless and unpoetical (when we leave its sublime history out of the question)," he then quotes a 300-word extract from *Tent Life in the Holy Land*, by William C. Prime (whom Twain calls "Wm. G. Grimes") extoling "the beauty of the scene." In what amounts to a guide book for careful reading, Twain then proceeds to deconstruct Primes' prose, or, as he puts it, to "strip from it" the "paint and the ribbons and the flowers" of rhetoric that make the passage so deceptive (509). Having exposed Prime's "Holy Land" as an illusion, Twain's narrator leads *his* reader back to the world that, he claims, is really there. While seldom this overt elsewhere, *Innocents Abroad* is repeatedly engaged in acts of unmasking what it variously treats as the "illusions" or "romantic dreams" or "deceptions" or even "frauds" that have been created and sustained by other writers. In Venice, his "cherished dreams" left in ruins by the sight and the smell of the stagnant, polluted canals, Twain acknowledges this process as a "system of destruction" (218). At times he can even imagine making the destruction real too: "If all the poetry and nonsense that have been discharged upon the fountains and the bland scenery of this region were collected in a book," he writes just before reaching the Sea of Galilee, "it would make a most valuable volume to burn" (495).

Romantic fictions aren't the only things Twain fantasizes about destroying. More than once he imagines taking violent revenge against reality for its failure to live up to his expectations. At a sufficient distance, for example, a group of Arabs gathered at a well near Nain evokes the "grand Oriental picture which I had worshiped a thousand times in soft, steel engravings." A nearer view reveals all that the picture left out, a list that ends with a bang: "no desolation; no dirt; no rags; no fleas; no ugly features; . . . no disagreeable jabbering in unknown tongues; no stench of camel; no suggestion that a couple of tons of powder placed under the party and touched off would heighten the effect . . ." (543–4). With "Mark Twain" it is always hard to know what really matters, and what is simply part of his rhetorical performance. We know that it had not really been his "cherished ambition to be shaved some day in a palatial barbershop in Paris" *from earliest infancy* – the hyperbole is part of the set-up to the schtick. Phrases like "which I had worshiped a thousand times" occur often in his account of visiting the biblical sites of the Holy Land. Throughout the trip he is devoutly cynical about Catholic and Muslem "superstitions," such "clap-trap side-shows and unseemly impostures of every kind" (573) as the hundreds of "pieces of the true cross" the pilgrims see in the cathedrals. But Twain never outgrew or finished coming to terms with his upbringing as a Protestant; among his late works are *Eve's Diary*, [Satan's] *Letters from the Earth*, and *Captain Stormfield's Visit to Heaven*. In Jerusalem he goes in person to the site of the crucifixion of Jesus, and describes his feelings this way: "I looked upon the place where the true cross once stood, with a far more absorbing interest than I had ever felt in any thing earthly before" (571).

In what could be read portentously as a very modern moment, Twain describes his "strange prospecting" at this site: what makes the deepest impression on him is the act of feeling around in the darkness of the "hole" in which the cross supposedly stood. Before the end of Twain's career, the next generation of American writers, Naturalists like Stephen Crane and Theodore Dreiser, would set their stories on the landscape adumbrated here, out of which the symbols that once gave meaning to life had vanished, leaving only the hole that their characters struggled to fill. The risk of the commitment that the Realists made to material circumstances, to what was "visible," "really there," was that actuality might not ultimately be able to satisfy the human need for larger meaning, for something to believe in. By setting themselves the project of un-writing romantic idealizations, they put themselves on a collision course with reality. There are other moments in Twain's encounter with the Holy Land that bring him to the verge of this incipient "waste land." At the scene of the Annunciation, for instance, he is shown the recess from which, according to the New Testament, the angel appeared to tell Mary she was pregnant with the savior of mankind; "I saw the little recess, . . . but could not fill its void" (527). In Bethlehem he confesses "I touch, with reverent finger, the actual spot where the infant Jesus lay, but I think – nothing" (601). Hole, void, nothing – it reads like a modern trinity. *Innocents Abroad* does not inhabit these moments for long, but even this first book of Twain's anticipates the pervasive sense of unreality and futility that he would eventually explore obsessively in the hundreds of pages of unfinished tales like "The Great Dark" and "The Mysterious Stranger."

More representative of *Innocents Abroad* as a whole, however, is the comic way he depicts his ostensible discovery of "the grave of Adam": in the tears of "filial affection" he claims to have shed for this "poor dead relative" (567), Twain mocks the cliches of sentimental voyagers like "Grimes," who "never bored but he struck water" (535), and makes the disparities between scriptural myths and concrete realities yield laughs instead of doubts. The scene of Twain crying at Adam's grave struck reviewers and readers in 1869 as hilarious; for many it became the book's signature moment, and Bliss shrewdly featured it in his advertising campaign. Modern readers, who do not share the cultural conditioning of the Americans in Twain's audience, are much less likely to laugh at this scene, or to easily understand why this first book remained his most popular book throughout his lifetime. Much of the cultural work that it did in its time by adopting an unabashedly new world perspective on the larger world, especially that Old World that Americans felt culturally inferior to, has already been done; "Mark Twain," for example, is now himself one of the world's treasured "Old Masters." And the book's comedy largely depends on habits of mind that no longer pervade the middle class that made it a best-seller. As stand-up comics know, people are likeliest to laugh when they are uncomfortable, and they become uncomfortable when the comedian brings up topics they have deep feelings about. Twain's irreverent behavior at Adam's grave was hilarious because his readers were so well versed and psychically invested in the reverent dis-courses of sentimentality and Christian piety. What was sacred to them, modern readers are often completely unfamiliar with, and so few in our time will have the experience to which the reviewers repeatedly bear witness: "in every paragraph," wrote *The Liberal Christian,* "you feel a giggle if you do not hear a laugh," while the Hartford *Courant* promised that "very few will be able to read it without laugh-ing at least half the time."[6]

The book which another reviewer called "wickedly amusing" pro-voked surprisingly little negative criticism, but Twain knew there was a crucial difference between making his readers uneasy enough to laugh and shocking their sensibilities. As he revised his original travel letters for book publication, he worked hard to "weed" them, as he put it in a letter to Emily Severance, of elements which, while they may have amused the western audience for whom he originally wrote, might alienate the more refined or fastidious taste of the largely eastern public he now saw himself performing for.[7] He eliminated a number of scenes, like an account of watching a group of nude bathers in Odessa, and a number of jokes – "Is it any wonder Christ walked?" he had written in the letter noting how much boatmen on the Sea of Galilee charged for carrying passengers – that threatened to cross the line between giving pleasure and giving offense. He eliminated entirely the character "Mr. Brown," a coarser vernacular figure who had been a kind of sidekick to "Mark Twain" in both the Sandwich Island and the *Quaker City* correspondence. He was careful to locate the "Mark Twain" persona itself inside the wider boundaries of middle class respectability as well as outside the narrow-minded priggishness of the "saints." "Mark Twain" is a man made entirely out of words, and he was careful to associate his voice with a linguistically acceptable vocabulary. When he heard that the San Francisco paper that had sponsored his trip proposed to bring out its own volume of them, for example, he hastily went west to prevent it: "If the *Alta*'s book were to come out with those wretched, slangy letters unrevised," he wrote Mrs. Fairbanks, "I should be utterly ruined."[8] The rhetorical anxiety displayed here led Twain to put all instances of slang or colloquial speech – words like "bully" and "cheek" – inside quotation marks, and often to add a remark in parentheses or a footnote to make sure his readers know he knows such language is frowned upon in respectable society.

For a writer, no question matters more than words, and as Twain's career went on he kept coming back to the issues of voice and diction. But for his audience in 1869, the most potentially disturbing aspect of *Innocents Abroad* was its representation of the Holy Land. As Twain's friend and one-time mentor Bret Harte put it in a review of the book: "There may be a question of taste in Mr. Clemens permitting such a man as 'Mark Twain' to go to the Holy Land at all."[9] Nearly everyone in his audience defined themselves as Christians, and would have rejected any attempt to see that land as anything *but* "Holy," to "leave its sublime history [as Twain put it when describing the scenery at Galilee] out of the question." In some respects, the ultimate "guide book" that is brought into question by Twain's actual experiences in the "Holy Land" is the Bible itself. But if Twain's greatest gift as a popular entertainer was exciting his audience's laughter, just as vital to his success was the talent to know when to stop. Later in his career he would let Huck Finn dismiss the lesson that the Widow tries to teach him out of "her book" (as Huck calls the Bible) once he finds out that Moses is dead: "I don't take no stock in dead people." Near the end of his career he found a way to rewrite one of the Bible's most sacred passages when, based on their experience with reality, the people of Hadleyburg revise the town's motto. But if *Innocents Abroad* continually challenges conventional proprieties, it seldom puts itself into radical opposition to them for long.

The recurring rhythm of the trip is to move from naive preconception to experiential disillusion to a form of recuperation. Venice, for example, seen from a distance, is "a great city, afloat on a placid sea, with its towers and domes and steeples drowsing in a golden mist of sunset" (216). Near at hand it is characterized by "poverty, neglect and melancholy decay," and its representative symbol is the "real" gondolier, "a mangy, barefooted gutter-snipe with a portion of his raiment [i.e. his underwear] on exhibition which should have been sacred from public scrutiny" (217–18). But two paragraphs later the sun goes down, "and under the mellow moonlight the Venice of poetry and romance stood revealed. . . . It was a beautiful picture – very soft and dreamy and beautiful" (218–19). Similarly, the passage "stripping" Galillee of its spirituality is not Twain's last word on that scene. Once again, "Night is the time to see Galilee": "In the starlight, Galilee . . . is a theatre meet for great events; meet for the birth of a religion able to save a world . . ." (512–13). This pattern of subverting and reassuring the ideological status quo reaches a kind of climax in his final words on the Holy Land, the two paragraphs summing up his pilgrimage:

> Palestine is desolate and unlovely. And why should it be otherwise? Can the *curse* of a Deity beautify a land?
>
> Palestine is no more of this work-day world. It is sacred to poetry and tradition – it is dream-land. (608)

Close readers might note the pervasive ambivalence: the first paragraph strips the poetical beauty out of the land, but retains "what is not visible," God's curse; the second seems to restore the ideal associations, but implies they are merely a hallucination. The book's original readers, however, agreed with the reviewer for the New Jersey *National Standard*, who recommended it as both "the raciest book we have met with" and safe: "its morals are of a high tone, and cannot be impeached."[10]

Because Twain's narrative ultimately allows its readers to hold on to their faiths, in Old World culture and in Christianity, the book's acts of irreverence are entertaining rather than revolutionary. When it comes to his audience's deepest ideological allegiances, Twain's narrator leaves no doubt that he is still one of "US"; he may disparage Catholicism and Islam as superstitions, but he overtly identifies himself with "the true religion – which is ours" (261). By "ours" he means the Protestant faith shared by over 90 percent of the United States at the time. He does not, however, go into more detail about this belief, and indeed the more he says, the more he is likely to estrange portions of his American audience. As it was, through the strategies he used to align "Mark Twain" with that audience, the book's irreverence becomes, as he wrote his publisher in early September, 1869, "a tip-top good feature of it <financially> diplomatically speaking."[11]

The humorist works in a very immediate medium: either the audience laughs or by its silence signals failure. In the delighted reviews of Twain's first book we can hear America laughing. Both financially and diplomatically *Innocents Abroad* was a hit with readers at home. Bliss' gamble in publishing a humorous subscription book paid off, and Twain's career as a popular writer was off to one of the best starts in American literary history.

2

Going West
Roughing It

Because of *Tom Sawyer* and *Huckleberry Finn*, most modern readers think of Mark Twain as a novelist. In his time, however, his travel books sold better than his fiction. Similarly, and also largely because of the books about Tom and Huck, we associate Twain with the Mississippi River and the middle of the continent. For at least the first ten years of his career, however, he was identified with the West, and labeled with nicknames like "the wild humorist of the Pacific Slope" or "the moralist of the [Spanish] Main." The reviewer of *Innocents Abroad* for the Hartford *Courant* spoke for his contemporaries when he said "Mark Twain is a true Californian."[1] Although Clemens only lived out west for five years altogether (less than two in California), this perception was consistent with the way the persona "Mark Twain" had been publicly shaped. He had been "born" on the frontier; his first nationally known work, "The Jumping Frog," is set in a California mining camp; in *Innocents Abroad* he identifies himself with the West, signing the preface "San Francisco," for example, and beginning the book's conclusion by saying "as I sit here at home in San Francisco."[2] Thus the reading public that had traveled east with him in *Innocents Abroad* was fully prepared to travel west with him in his next book, *Roughing It*.

An account of his travels and adventures between 1861 and 1866 in Nevada, California, and Hawaii, *Roughing It* was published in 1872, three years after *Innocents*. If we look at Twain's life during the years between the Holy Land excursion and the book's publication, it exposes the unreality of that phrase "at home in San Francisco." He did make one brief visit to the West in 1868, to secure exclusive rights to his *Alta* correspondence, but after that trip he never saw California or Nevada again. In fact, Twain had been moving steadily in the opposite direction, both geographically – by 1872, in fact, he was a resident of Hartford – and socially: by 1872 he was at least literally "at home" amidst the elegancies, refinements and repressions of upper class gentility. In one of his last letters to the *Alta*, Twain himself called his western rags to eastern riches story a fairy tale come true: "I have *read* those absurd fairy tales in my time, but I never, never, never, expected to be the hero of a romance in real life."[3] The heroine of this romance was Olivia Langdon, whose picture, so the story goes, Twain fell in love with the instant her brother Charley showed it to him while they were roommates on the *Quaker City*. He met her in person when Charley invited him to spend an evening with the family in New York City at Christmas, 1867. She was 27, shy, a semi-invalid, and astonished at the determined ardor with which the older (he was 33) and much more worldly Clemens courted her. After a stay in the Langdon mansion in Elmira, New York, that Twain extended as long as he could, he first proposed to Livy in early September, 1868.

She said No, but promised to continue their relationship as apprentice and master – he was the apprentice, she was the master, and the training was intended to make a Christian gentleman of him. Reading *The Love Letters of Mark Twain*, as one collection of them is entitled, can unsettle fans of his irreverence: she sent him Henry Ward Beecher's sermons and a Bible that she had annotated for him, and he wrote back scores of long letters to say "I love to follow your teachings. Every day in my little Testament I track you by your pencil through your patient search for that wisdom that adorns you so much."[4] To satisfy her desire for his reformation, he swore to give up profanity and alcohol, and came close to promising to quit smoking. Huck found this kind of regimen intolerable after the Widow adopted him, but Twain submitted to it patiently until, first, Livy said Yes (that happened in November), then the Langdon family accepted him (after getting very mixed reports on his character from Mrs. Fairbanks and his former acquaintances in California, they capitulated in January, 1869), and finally, in February 1870, he and Livy were married. His courtship letters may have been entirely sincere, or the part of supplicant prodigal may have been another rhetorical persona designed to ingratiate himself with an audience – consisting, in this case, of Livy and her family. The letter Sam wrote to his own family in Missouri to announce his engagement supports either interpretation: "[Livy] said she never could or would love me – but she set herself the task of making a Christian of me. I said she would succeed, but that in the meantime she would unwittingly dig a matrimonial pit & end by tumbling into it."[5]

Twain never did become a Christian, nor gave up swearing and drinking, but with his marriage he found a source of domestic happiness that failed only when death parted him from his oldest daughter (in 1896) and his wife (in 1904). His marriage also made him one of the "elect" socio-economically. Livy was the daughter of Jervis Langdon, a one-time storekeeper who had made a fortune in coal. They cautiously accepted Twain as a son-in-law, but made sure that he could keep Livy in the style she was accustomed to. Before the marriage Langdon loaned him $12,500 to buy into *The Express*, a newspaper in nearby Buffalo. On his wedding night Twain discovered that the Langdons had also bought the newlyweds a house in a fashionable Buffalo neighborhood, and stocked it with furniture, and hired three servants who, as he wrote a childhood friend just four days after the wedding, "respectfully call us 'Mr.' and 'Mrs. Clemens.'"[6] Twain was ready to become accustomed to this life: "It took me many a year to work up to where I can put on style," he told his friend, "but now I'll do it." He dated this letter "At Home," but in fact never managed to get comfortable in Buffalo and soon determined to sell the house. In October, 1871, he moved his family and servants still further east and further upward, to the aristocratic Nook Farm neighborhood in the more fashionable city of Hartford. There he lived for the next two decades. Except for the years he spent living in Europe, Twain spent the rest of his life in the northeast putting on the style of the gentleman of wealth.

I have been saying "Twain," but of course the life I am describing was being lived by "Mr. and Mrs. Clemens." What about "Mark Twain"? Where was he "at home"? After the success of his first subscription book left no doubt in his or his publisher's mind that there should be a second, he decided imaginatively to return to the West. In the summer of 1870 he began writing an account of his experiences ten years earlier, when he accompanied his brother Orion to the territory of Nevada. That may remind us of Huck's decision to "light out" westward rather than allow Aunt Sally to "sivilize" him, but little in the book he wrote suggests that "Mark Twain" felt any more "at home" in the American West than he had in the Old World. As in *Innocents Abroad*, the story he tells in *Roughing It* is that of a stranger in a strange land. Alighting from the stagecoach in Overland City, the first western town he and Orion reach, sounds like landing on a different planet: "We tumbled out [of the stage] into the busy street feeling like meteoric people crumbled off the corner of some other world, and wakened up suddenly in this" (42).

There are several different ways to appreciate the distance the narrative maintains between its first-person protagonist and the environment through which he moves. At this early point in his career, Twain is still constructing his image, and as in *Innocents* he carefully keeps his "I" within the standards of bourgeois gentility. His description of the first Overland station they stop at fastidiously remarks the absence of such tokens of respectability as "table-cloth and napkins" (23) and notes that he was obliged to sit "at the same board" with the "low, rough characters" (37) who work for the stage company. This class consciousness is maintained throughout – when a flash flood strands him for a week at Honey Lake Smith's tavern, he resents being "cooped up" with "that curious crew" (200) – but not always maintained this primly. He glories, for example, in "the wild sense of freedom" of traveling by stagecoach, including the chance to strip down to one's underclothes (29–30). When much later he evokes the spirit of the vanished mining towns, he can sound like Walt Whitman celebrating the roughs: "It was an assemblage of two hundred thousand *young* men – not simpering, dainty, kid-gloved weaklings, but stalwart, muscular, dauntless young braves, brim full of push and energy, and royally endowed with every attribute that goes to make up a peerless and magnificent manhood" (391–2). But although the book is the record of his travels further and further into the west, he never depicts himself as being transformed by the journey: he is in the frontier, but not of it; among the roughs, but never one of them. As always in Twain's works, words are decisive, and the language of the narrator remains consistently segregated from "the vigorous new vernacular of the occidental plains and mountains" (26). By "vernacular" he means the slang that gives the voices of the miners and prospectors such force, but by his own use of words like "vernacular" and "occidental" he maintains his credentials as refined, cultured, civilized. As in *Innocents*, all the slang in *Roughing It* is inside quotation marks.

While Twain was anxious to be identified with his middle class audience, he was most concerned to entertain it. As an outsider, he can continue to cast himself in the part of naif, the tenderfoot whose innocence becomes the occasion for all kinds of misadventures. He sets up this pose on the book's very first page, where on the verge of going into the west he describes himself as "young and ignorant" and someone who "never had been away from home" – although of course he had not lived at home for many years, and had spent the last four as a riverboat pilot (1). The night before the trip begins, he says, he spent dreaming about "hav[ing] all kinds of adventures" among "Indians, deserts and silver bars" (2). These are like the dreams in *Innocents* of being sensuously shaved in Paris or luxuriating in a Turkish bath: destined to be exploded by realities. For many readers the signature scene of *Roughing It* is his adventure in chapter 24 with "a Genuine Mexican Plug" (159). Having "quickly learned to tell a horse from a cow," he tells us, he is impatient to own one so he can imitate the "picturesquely-clad Mexicans, Californians and Mexicanized-Americans" he sees galloping through Carson City. "You are a stranger," says the man on the street who convinces him to buy the Plug that is being auctioned. As a stranger, there is a lot he doesn't know: for instance, that his advisor is really the auctioneer's brother. Nor does he know what a "plug" is, or even what "bucking" means. But he finds out once he buys the horse and tries to ride it. For those readers who do not already know the fate of such innocence in Twain's texts, True Williams' illustration of the scene in the original edition should say it all (see Figure 2).

Twain never tries riding the Plug again, but he does repeatedly re-enact this process of losing his innocence. In places the pattern resembles the un-writing project of *Innocents* closely, as when the narrator compares his fantasies as a former "disciple of Cooper and a worshipper of the Red Man – even of the scholarly savages in the 'Last of the Mohicans'" with the squalid "Indians" he encounters a couple weeks into the trip (129). But *Roughing It* is not so thematically coherent as the earlier book. The protagonist's naivete, established at the start by his character as a "young and ignorant" outsider, is essentially just a comic resource that never fails. He is no more adept at picking out and riding a horse in Hawaii (chapters 64–5) than he had been in Nevada, no more adept at prospecting than at finding his way through a snow storm (chapters 28, 31–3 and so on). Even when he reaches

UNEXPECTED ELEVATION.

FIGURE 2   Illustration by True Williams for page 180, *Roughing It*
(Hartford: American Publishing Company, 1872)

the point at which he becomes a professional writer, he keeps emphasizing his ineptitudes and misfortunes. If the outsider ever described himself as an insider, the opportunity for the kind of humor on which the narrative depends would be gone. Even at the end of what (before the journey west begins) he calls "six or seven uncommonly long years" (2), he remains a tenderfoot.

At the same time, the motif of the outsider has serious resonances in Twain's work. A travel writer, of course, is by definition never "at home," but even some of his best known fictions originate in situations involving extreme strangeness – a prince, for example, who abruptly finds himself a pauper, locked out of the palace he had called home. Twain's Connecticut Yankee awakens to find himself not just thousands of miles but also thirteen centuries away from the world he knew, and Hank Morgan never does make it back home. By the end of his story he has returned to the 19th century, but dies "a stranger and forlorn" in a strange land, indeed dies, the narrative suggests, of strangeness.[7] The story Twain kept trying to finish in the last decade of his career is the one we know as "The Mysterious Stranger," about a non-human being who comes to earth from another world entirely. Although he had become one of the most world's most familiar inhabitants, shortly before he died Twain told his biographer about his kinship with Haley's Comet: he and this interplanetary wanderer were a pair of "unaccountable freaks" who "came in together" and "must go out together."[8] In fact, the Comet had been visible in the heavens when Sam Clemens was born in 1835, and its 75-year orbit had brought it back to earth's skies when Mark Twain died in 1910. Whatever else the coincidence might mean, Twain's sense of twinship with this cosmic outsider, this stranger from a distance that can only be measured in astronomical units, suggests how deep and abiding was his sense of alienation, his feeling of being (as he put it in that passage about arriving in Overland City) "like meteoric people crumbled off the corner of some other world."

There's another facet of Twain's personality marked by his choice of Haley's Comet as *his* sign – his hunger for fame. Even the biggest star shares the night sky, but the comet blazes alone at the center of every onlooker's attention. *Roughing It* is the work of a very ambitious man who disguises his hunger behind the pose of innocence, and who ultimately, paradoxically, succeeds by failing so unfailingly. *Roughing It* is an anti-success story, a parodic revision of the culturally sanctioned process summed up by the advice commonly attributed to Horace Greeley: "Go west, young man, and grow up with the country." Greeley himself appears twice in Twain's book: in chapter 20 we hear about the knocking around he takes while traveling out west himself, and in chapter 70 we watch someone driven mad by trying to decipher Greeley's advice to another young man. *Roughing It* can be read as the misadventures of a young man who goes west and keeps falling down as the country grows up around him. His "long array of failures" (273) reaches a climax in the middle when he and his friend Higbie hit paydirt by finding a treasure-bearing "blind lead" underground in chapter 40 – "I was worth a million dollars" (260) – only to discover in chapter 41 that thanks to another piece of ineptitude "I was a pauper now" (266). But this is only the most dramatic instance of the pattern of promise and bankruptcy, dream and disillusionment, that is repeated throughout; "it was the blind lead come again" becomes a refrain (379, 403). He fails as a timberman (he burns the woods down), prospector, day-laborer, stock speculator; he even fails as a writer: as a newspaper editor in Nevada and a reporter in San Francisco.

Two chapters from the end, returning to San Francisco after six months in the Sandwich Islands, he still finds himself "without means and without employment" (533). At this point the "saving scheme" that occurs to him, apparently from nowhere, is to give "a public lecture." This time his anticipatory dreams are of disaster ("I would make a humiliating failure," "[I] was the most distressed and frightened creature on the Pacific coast") while in reality the stand-up routine about "Our Fellow Savages of the Sandwich Islands" that he delivers to a packed crowd at "the new opera-house" is a triumph, and he finds a career for himself as a performer. The "Mark Twain" persona seems finally to have found a home: in friendly faces of the "house," as live audiences are called, he finds the means to make himself "comfortable, and even content" (535). The crowd and the reviewers are delighted, and at last he can end a chapter saying "I had abundance of money" (536). In the final chapter he describes himself successfully "launched" on the first of "Mark Twain's" many lecture tours. This enables him to return to the Nevada territory, scene of his earlier misfortunes, and find a source of gold and silver that would never fail him: the public appetite for his entertaining humor.

He is careful not to ruin the narrative's design by turning it into too glowing a success story. In keeping with the comically inept persona he has created, he makes himself the butt of his own success that first night in San Francisco: the audience's biggest laugh, "the triumph of the evening," comes inadvertently in response to the one "bit of serious matter" in his lecture (536). He allows the book's readers to smile as his discomfiture even as he acknowledges the way he made that live audience roar. And the very last incident he recounts leaves him looking ridiculous to an "audience" inside as well as outside the book. While walking back at midnight from a sold-out lecture in Gold Hill to his hotel in Virginia City, he is waylaid by a gang of armed masked men who take back the profits of his performance and leave the celebrity standing alone in the dark with his hands up, afraid to move, for ten minutes. "Now this whole thing was a practical joke," he lets us know while he describes himself standing there, "and the robbers were personal friends . . . and twenty more lay hidden within ten feet of us during the whole operation, listening" (540). By the time he is let in on the joke, his nightime exposure has resulted in "a troublesome disease" (541) that sustains the book's anti-success motif even in its account of "Mark Twain" as a rising star. According to the story Roughing It tells, and especially the one it implies through these concluding episodes, "exciting the laughter of God's creatures" gave Twain a way to convert misfortune into a fortune – but there is a crucial difference between popularity and precious metals as a means of making it in America. You cannot put popularity in the bank; it has to be continually renewed at its source; the successful entertainer remains in some ways always at the mercy of his audience.

As itself a performance for an audience of readers, Roughing It re-enacts much the same drama of self-consciousness. Traveling through America, for example, puts him rhetorically on more dangerous ground than taking on the Old World; it is one thing to make Italian Catholics and Arab villagers look silly, as Innocents Abroad had done, but riskier to ask an American audience to laugh at American subjects. Twain published two travel books with American settings. Before publishing Life on the Mississippi (1883), he went through his manuscript and deleted almost every passage that could be construed as satirical or critical about his reading public's culture.[9] In Roughing It, the targets of his irreverence are almost invariably versions of the "Other," people whom middle class readers would see as essentially as foreign as

Italians or Arabs. There are four chapters on the Mormons (13–16) making fun of polygamy and the Mormon Bible. The chapter on the "Chinese population" in the West (chapter 54) contains several pointed critiques of how they are discriminated against, but ends with a visit to a "Chinatown" full of stereotypes – including an addict whose opium dream "we could not imagine by looking at the soggy creature" (373) – and a disclaimer that protects his audience: "No California *gentleman or lady* ever abuses or oppresses a Chinaman . . . Only the scum of the population do it" (375). And Twain's representation of the Native American population is savagely racist. His repeated disparagements of them culminate in his description of the Goshoot Indians in chapter 19 as "the wretchedest type of mankind I have ever seen," then the generalizing of this contempt to all Native Americans: "wherever one finds an Indian tribe he has only found Goshoots more or less modified" (126, 129).

Again in the Sandwich Island chapters (63–76), although he includes several sarcastic digs at the negative effects of the coming of Christian civilization and its missionaries – "contact with civilization," he notes, "has reduced the native population from *four hundred thousand* . . . to *fifty-five thousand* in something over eighty years" (454) – on the whole he keeps his narrative focused on those "Others," and such exotic curiosities as their "barbarian superstitions" (458) and their "dusky maidens" (460). In the 19th century there were essentially two different plot lines for telling about the transformation of peoples labeled "savage" by processes labeled "civilized": the story of a fall from an edenic innocence, or of a progress upward toward a truer faith and a superior culture. Twain's account of that process leaves plenty of room for both interpretations. "The benefit conferred on this [native] people by the missionaries is so prominent," he says at the end of chapter 64, that "Their work speaks for itself" (441). Perhaps it speaks ironically of a tragic loss; *he* is clearly speaking ironically when he says he is "sad to think of the multitudes who have gone to their graves in this beautiful island and never knew there was a hell!" (440) Most contemporary readers, however, probably heard implied what he told that lecture audience overtly: that as the Islands' native population vanishes, "we will take possession as lawful heirs."[10] "Manifest destiny" was the slogan under which the United States had marched across the continent to the Pacific; like the California paper that sent him to report on Hawaii, Twain projects that doctrine further westward, into the Pacific.

Thirty years later, at the start of the 20th century, in response to America's colonization of the Philipine Islands, Twain announced that he was "an anti-imperialist": "I am opposed to having the eagle put its talons on any other land."[11] The stance Twain took at that time in articles like "To the Person Sitting in Darkness" (1901) and "King Leopold's Soliloquy" (1905) constitutes the last major phase of his public career, when he used his ironist's wit and his popular status to protest against the West's oppression of what we now call the Third World. His commitment to this cause first emerges in his last travel book, *Following the Equator* (1897); his trip around the world gives him many opportunities to witness the interactions between the outposts of the British Empire and the native populations in Australia, New Zealand, India and South Africa. In passages like the following he is making a new kind of joke: "There are many humorous things in the world; among them the white man's notion that he is less savage than the other savages."[12]

The image of Twain standing up for the oppressed added to his stature as a voice for democratic values, but it is important to note whom he is standing up against. Even in this late works, he condemns most aggressively European imperial powers, especially Germany and Belgium; he also attacks President McKinley as "the Master" whose international policy imitates the corrupt "European game" rather than "the regular *American* game" he should be playing;[13] even that distinction, however, protects his audience from any culpability for what the United States is doing. As an anti-imperialist polemicist, he confronted world leaders but not his readers. And the reader of *Roughing It* could only conclude that the nation's westward expansion into the "Indian territories," which historians now understand as a form of imperialism, is a moral imperative. Between the time Clemens left the west and Twain published the book, the transcontinental railroad had been completed, but the country was still fighting the Indian Wars by which the subjugation of Native Americans was militarily enforced. The book's representation of the Indians leaves no room for doubting that their displacement from the landscape by the actions of soldiers and settlers is right. This is one of the most important ideological services that Twain's second book performed for his contemporaries: while *Innocents Abroad* goes east to emancipate them from the European past, *Roughing It* helps legitimize winning the west as the (white) American future.

Although *Roughing It* is organized around the juxtaposition between eastern society and the frontier west, it puts surprisingly little dialectic pressure on the preconceptions of "the eastern reader" for whom it is written (60). The book's most suggestive scene dramatizes the conflict between these two cultures, but in a way that clearly indicates the narrative's ultimate allegiances. Chapter 47 recounts the conversation between "Scotty" Briggs, a "stalwart rough" from "the vast bottom-stratum of [Virginia City] society," and a greenhorn minister, "a fragile, gentle, spirituel new fledgling from an eastern theological seminary" (308–9). Death brings them together: they meet to arrange a funeral for Buck Fanshaw, Scotty's best friend and fellow "rough." Their lives have kept them very far apart. They have been shaped by antithetical environments – Scotty among the realities of the frontier, the minister among the ideals of Christianity – and therefore speak almost two entirely different languages. Scotty asks if the minister is "the duck that runs the gospel-mill next door"; the minister says that he is "the shepherd in charge of the flock whose fold is next door." In this kind of collision between a colloquial vernacular rooted in personal experience and a formal language founded on abstractions derived from books, Twain regularly finds not just humorous misunderstandings but one of his central themes as a realist. Potentially, there are profound issues at stake in this encounter. Which man lives closer to the meaning of life? "Was he a good man" is what the minister wants to know about Buck. Scotty thinks he understands the question, but his western notion of "good" is not at all the definition that the minister brought with him from that eastern seminary: "Pard," says Scotty, "you would have doted on that man. He could lam any galoot of his inches in America. . . . He could run faster, jump higher, hit harder, and hold more tangle-foot whisky without spilling it than any man in seventeen counties." In *Huck Finn* this tension – between written and oral, abstract and concrete, genteel and vernacular, allegorical and existential – remains powerfully unresolved. Scotty and the minister, though, find common ground in Buck's conventionally sentimental relationship with his mother, and Twain winds up privileging the minister's (and his own audience's) eastern values when Scotty becomes a "convert" to Christianity. Our last glimpse of him is as a Sunday School class leader, teaching "his pioneer small fry" – the territory's next generation – "the beautiful story of Joseph and his brethren." His diction remains "riddled with slang," but he now serves as a spokesman for devoutly respectable society, or what, in its last words, the chapter calls "the sacred proprieties."

In fact, before letting us hear Scotty's voice, Twain set up the encounter by establishing a genteel point-of-view as the narrative's ultimate perspective: "in after days," the anecdote begins, "it was worth something to hear the minister tell about it [i.e. his meeting with Scotty]." The line between east and west has been sharply (and humorously) drawn, but in this Twain text west meets east on the terms laid down by the east. Making the minister the authoritative source pre-empts the possibility that Scotty's existential, vernacular code of meaning and behavior might in any way transform the civilization that the minister, like those missionaries in Hawaii, travels as an agent for. The famous "frontier thesis" that Frederick Jackson Turner elaborated two decades after Twain's book was published held that "the colonization of the Great West" fundamentally reshaped the preconceptions settlers brought with them from Europe, that the "expansion westward with its new opportunities . . . furnish[ed] the forces dominating American character."[14] Twain, however, ultimately treats the frontier of *Roughing It* more as a phase through which society passes on its way back to that point from which, as a matter of fact, he set out to remember his earlier life in the west: the point represented by the genteel world he inhabited as Olivia Langdon's husband, doing his best, like Scotty in Sunday School, to behave according to eastern standards. As an "American character," the "Mark Twain" of *Roughing It* seems largely unshaped by the frontier.

Twain's text, however, does open up an idea of the "West" that remains vital long after the frontier, as Turner noted, closed in 1890. This "West" exists imaginatively rather than literally, and is brought into being each time Twain's episodic narrative pauses to listen to someone tell a tall tale. There are half a dozen of these scattered through the book, from Bemis' account of the buffalo that chased him up into a tree (chapter 7) to the celebrated "lies" of a man named Markiss, including the story of John Godfrey working for "the Incorporated Company of Mean Men" (chapter 77). Several of these – Jim Blaine and his grandfather's ram (chapter 53), or Dick Baker and his cat (chapter 61) – have often been excerpted into anthologies as classic examples of Twain's humor. The energy in these tales is largely created by the colloquial voices we hear telling them, and the joy they provide derives largely from the matter-of-fact tone in which they are told: behind both the down-to-earth diction and the deadpan tone lies the "West" as a space large enough to make such "tall" impossibilities seem ordinary. William Dean Howells captured this sense in his review of *Roughing It*: "The grotesque exaggeration and broad irony with which life is described are conjecturably the truest colors that could have been used, for all existence there ['the recent West'] must have looked like an extravagant joke."[15] It is a joke that the text invites everyone to share, from the vernacular story-tellers who are the "Old Masters" of this oral culture, to the eastern readers whose only access to their art is a book. Even the narrator is "at home" in this imaginative west, the land of opportunity for the humorous imagination. He tells the first tall tale himself, in chapter 3, in an anecdote that starts off describing what camels are capable of eating and ends by implicitly asking its readers how much they can swallow. "In Syria, once" – thus it begins – he watched a camel devour one of his coats until it found his "newspaper correspondence" in one of the pockets. The camel "began to gag and gasp," and finally "choked to death on one of the mildest and gentlest statements of fact that I ever laid before a trusting public" (15–17). It is a great way to start his second book: the Holy Land setting reminds his contemporary audience of the pleasure they found in *Innocents Abroad*; the issues of gullability and reliability serve as our initiation into the realm of *Roughing It*, where the narrator will be taken in again and again, but at the same time will succeed by taking in his readers. And this dynamic of being taken in makes everyone an outsider and an insider together. The freedom of both the "West" and the text is from the need for truth: in the borderless space opened up each time a story is begun, the treasure is found in letting oneself be taken for the ride.

Going Home
Tom Sawyer

The Adventures of Tom Sawyer, like all Twain's subscription books, was published with lots of illustrations. Most were the work of True Williams, who was the main illustrator for *Innocents Abroad* and *Roughing It* too. One picture, however, was almost certainly drawn by Twain himself: the chalk-on-school-slate "caricature of a house" that Tom creates to attract Becky Thatcher's attention (see figure 3).[1] We might have expected Tom to imagine an outlaw in the woods or a pirate on the ocean. A large house, a lady (note the fan), a gentleman (note the top hat) – at first this scene seems (like so much of Twain's art) more calculated to satisfy its audience's expectations than to express its artist's spirit. Becky's attention is fully caught: "It's ever so nice," she tells Tom (55). But although we like to remember Tom as a kind of rebel – playing hookey, climbing out of windows, running away – the novel also associates him with the values of genteel respectability displayed in his drawing. On the list of things he plans to do once he and Huck find buried treasure are buy "a red tie" and "get married" (178), and when in Sunday School he first sees Becky's father, the rich and prominent Judge Thatcher, Tom's first impulse is "to fall down and worship him" (35). The picture Tom draws for Becky is also the future he plans for Huck, when at the novel's end he orders his friend to go back to the Widow's big house and learn to be "respectable," because "everybody does that" (258, 257). The picture also reveals a lot about what mattered to the man who originally drew it, whether we call him Mark Twain or Samuel Clemens.

To a live entertainer, like Twain on one of his lecture tours, "house" is a technical term meaning the people in the audience. The narrator

"Let me see it."

Tom partly uncovered a dismal caricature of a house with two gable ends to it and a cork-screw of smoke issuing from the chimney. Then the girl's interest began to fasten itself upon the work and she forgot everything else. When it was finished, she gazed a moment, then whispered:

"It's nice—make a man."

The artist erected a man in the front yard, that resembled a derrick. He could have stepped over the house; but the girl was not hypercritical; she was satisfied with the monster, and whispered:

"It's a beautiful man—now make me coming along."

Tom drew an hour-glass with a full moon and straw limbs to it and armed the

TOM AS AN ARTIST.

spreading fingers with a portentous fan. The girl said:

"It's ever so nice—I wish I could draw."

"It's easy," whispered Tom, "I'll learn you."

"O, will you? When?"

"At noon. Do you go home to dinner?"

"I'll stay if you will."

"Good,— that's a whack. What's your name?"

"Becky Thatcher. What's yours? Oh, I know. It's Thomas Sawyer."

"That's the name they lick me by. I'm Tom when I'm good. You call me Tom, will you?"

"Yes."

Now Tom began to scrawl something on the slate, hiding the words from the girl. But she was not backward this time. She begged to see. Tom said:

"Oh it ain't anything."

"Yes it is."

"No it ain't. You don't want to see."

FIGURE 3   Drawing by Mark Twain for page 70, *The Adventures of Tom Sawyer* (Hartford: American Publishing Company, 1875)

of *Tom Sawyer* uses the word that way to refer to the congregation in church (130), the community at a school assembly (155), the public in a courtroom (170), and so on. As a compulsive performer, Twain was anxious throughout his career to have a "good house." At the stage of Clemens' life when *Tom Sawyer* was written, a good house also had a particularly keen literal significance. Two years after moving from Buffalo to Hartford in 1871, he and Livy purchased a five-acre lot next to Harriet Beecher Stowe's home in the exclusive Nook Farm neighborhood and began building what Howells called a "palace of a house."[2] Twain began writing *Tom Sawyer* in the summer of 1874, right in the middle of this house's construction; by that fall, before either the house or the novel was finished, he and his growing family and their servants, at times as many as seven, had moved in. Twain loved the house as a symbol of his success, but it quickly became apparent that with this move he had mortgaged his life and imagination to a style of living that would tax even his earning power; as he wrote Howells in the summer of 1875, just after finishing *Tom Sawyer*, "my household expenses are something almost ghastly."[3] In fact, to save money he would often have to close the house up, which explains why between 1875 and 1900 he spent over 10 years living in Europe. In that summer of 1874, however, he moved no further than Elmira, New York, where his wife's older sister had built a study for him on top of a hill looking down on a river, and it was there that he took an imaginative flight from his status as husband, father, and parvenu member of New England's aristocracy. Although Sam Clemens had run away from the world of his childhood at the earliest possible moment, now, as Mark Twain, he decided to go back to it: to transform his memories of growing up in Hannibal into Tom's adventures in a village named St Petersburg.

Howells wrote the first review of *Tom Sawyer*. Although usually an astute critic, Howells was surely wrong to call the novel "realistic in the highest degree."[4] That adjective, however, does provide a way to locate the novel, the first Twain wrote on his own,[5] in the larger context of Twain's career. It was as a realist that he had written sketches about a "Good Boy" and a "Bad Boy" in the 1860s; as we noted in chapter 1, he often created his texts as burlesque or parodic re-writings of conventional discourse. He was probably thinking along similar lines when he started *Tom Sawyer*: by pointing out that his protagonist was "not the Model Boy of the village" (5), for example,

Twain subversively contrasts Tom with the type of Exemplary Hero who appeared in didactic tales intended to enlighten and improve young readers; Louisa May Alcott's *Little Women* (1868) and its sequels are the best-known, and the best, examples of these books, which were, whatever the kids thought of them, so popular with parents and other adults in the 19th century. Twain also has a lot of fun, especially in the first half of the novel, using his juvenile lovers Tom and Becky to mock the trials of the typical romance hero and heroine. But finally very little of the power of *Tom Sawyer* is derived from such acts of comic deconstruction, nor is "reality" the story's ultimate point of reference. *Tom Sawyer* is Twain's most fully sustained fantasy, his most devout act of re-creation, or, to use his phrase for it, "simply a hymn."[6]

Hymns stand at the opposite end of the aesthetic spectrum from the genres Twain usually works in: his writing tends to be irreverent, funny and devoted to materiality; hymns are worshipful, serious and most especially, spiritual and idealistic. Hymns are a means for people to try to transcend reality, to make contact with an unseen, higher world that has the power to both give meaning to and save them from the world they actually live in. In *Tom Sawyer*, childhood is such a world. The novel's opening scene is very delicately balanced between the skeptical and the scriptural. Actually, the text that is being un-written here *is* Scripture: the Genesis account of the forbidden fruit becomes Tom's adventure with the jam that Aunt Polly has forbidden him to eat. His first act in the novel is to eat of this jam, but while he arouses Polly's wrath, he escapes all her attempts at punishment, and his engaging disobedience becomes the portal through which the reader is led into the paradisical kingdom of childhood. *Tom Sawyer* replaces the doctrine of the Fall with the vision of an eternal summer where, in fact, the penalties of the Fall seem no longer to be enforced. Take work, for instance. In Eden there was no need to labor, but as part of Adam's punishment for having sinned, God tells him, "In the sweat of thy brow shalt thy eat bread, till thy return unto the ground" (Genesis 3:19). "I'll be just obleeged to make him work, to-morrow, to punish him" is how Aunt Polly puts it to herself after catching Tom with jam on his face (3). Sure enough, the next day, Saturday, she resolutely gives him the job of white-washing the fence. But of course this leads to what is probably the novel's single best-known scene, as Tom comes up with a strategy that not only allows him to rest while the other boys "worked and sweated in the sun," but also cons them into paying him for the privilege: "when the middle of the afternoon came, from being a poor poverty-stricken boy in the morning, Tom was literally rolling in wealth" (15).

With this scene one of the book's central patterns is established: in the world of *Tom Sawyer* most of the evils that cause mankind so much suffering are dispelled. For another instance, take money. The "wealth" that Tom acquires by "bankrupt[ing] every boy in the village" consists of such things as "a tin soldier, a couple of tadpoles, six fire-crackers" – there is no danger that gaining this kind of money will corrupt him, nor will the want of it cause the other boys any evil. The most astonishing of the victories that the novel wins over suffering concerns another of the penalties of the Fall from Eden: "on the day that thou eatest" of the forbidden fruit, God warns Adam, "thou shalt surely die" (Genesis 2:17). In this novel, however, death has no dominion. Early on, feeling unloved and misunderstood, Tom expresses the outrageous wish that he might be able to "die *temporarily!*" (64). Less than ten chapters later, that wish comes true when all the people of St Petersburg, believing Tom and Joe Harper have drowned, gather in church at a funeral service for the boys. After remaining "dead" long enough to hear how much he is missed, Tom performs his own resurrection, transforming his funeral into "the proudest moment in his life" (131). In *Tom Sawyer* Twain renames the village of Hannibal "St Petersburg"; as many appreciative readers have noted, there is something heavenly about that name, just as there is something redemptive about the way the narrative transforms childhood into a miraculous series of adventures set in an eternal summer under a sun that "beamed down upon the peaceful village like a benediction" (26).

As a child, Sam Clemens was an avid reader of Walter Scott and Fenimore Cooper. *The Adventures of Tom Sawyer* proves what a gifted romance writer he might have become, for the kinds of wishes that his narrative fulfills belong equally to the make-believe of children and the conventions of romance. The main story-line of the book's second half is launched when Tom abruptly decides "to go somewhere and dig for hidden treasure." As the narrator sententiously informs us, this impulse is one that appears "in every rightly constructed boy's life" (175); as Twain constructs his boy's story, however, Tom not only *looks* for treasure – he actually *finds* it. (It is probably no coincidence, given how much money Twain was pouring into his new Hartford residence as he wrote the book, that the fortune is found in an old house.) Similarly, Tom and Huck not only go to a graveyard at midnight to see the devil – their vigil is rewarded with an adventure that is both incredibly exciting and generically conventional. They witness a murder at midnight in a cemetery by the revengeful half-breed "Injun Joe." In *Roughing It* Twain had realistically debunked Cooper's literary "Indians," but "Injun Joe" is a stereotype that has been derived directly from the kinds of stock figures Cooper's fictions dealt in. In fact, in the way that *Tom Sawyer* casts Joe in the role of a quasi-gothic villain who haunts the darkness we see how Twain is using romance conventions to preserve the enchantment of his imagined world: just as the Hero will always rescue the Heroine, so will the violence be safely contained inside stock scenes (graveyards at midnight) and projected onto an archetypical Villain (the vengeful "Injun").

For the most part in *Tom Sawyer* Twain keeps the world he had grown up in at a distance, like Cardiff Hill, which "lay just far enough away to seem a Delectable Land, dreamy, reposeful and inviting" (10). In his travel books such beguiling vistas often prove false on nearer approach, and there are moments in the novel when the enchantment is threatened by the facts of life in "the poor little shabby village" (5). We can take work again, for example. Mr Dobbins, St Petersburg's school teacher, finds nothing adventurous in the way he is forced to earn his bread: he "had reached middle age with an unsatisfied ambition. The darling of his desires was, to be a doctor, but poverty had decreed that he should be nothing higher than a village school-master" (149). Money looks much less playful when at the end we learn that after Tom found his treasure, lots of other old houses have been torn apart, "and not by boys, but men – pretty grave, unromantic men, too, some of them" (254). And death looks much less temporary in the narrative's brief but vivid description of the village graveyard: "grass and weeds grew rank . . . the old graves were sunken in . . . round-topped, worm-eaten boards staggered over the graves, leaning for support and finding none. 'Sacred to the memory of So-and-so' had been painted on them once, but it could no longer [be] read" (71–2). But almost without exception, such quotidian disillusionments are associated with adults, in whose company the narrative spends very little time – just long enough, in fact, to make child's play shine in comparison to the dull frustrations of adulthood.

The Adventures of Tom Sawyer is categorized as a classic children's book. Twain himself, who was almost forty years old when he wrote the novel, did not think of it that way: "It is *not* a boy's book, at all," he wrote Howells immediately after finishing the manuscript; "It will only be read by adults. It was only written for adults."[7] It was actually Howells, to whom he sent the manuscript for his suggestions, who convinced Twain that *Tom Sawyer* should be marketed as a book for young readers. Curiously, the publicity material that Bliss sent his subscription agents in 1875 contains no hint of this design. By the 1890s, however, *Tom Sawyer* was being sold in bookstores, where buyers have always been most likely to find it in the children's section. There is no doubt that generations of young readers have been entertained by the story. Scenes like the white-washing episode are victories over tedium and authority and even reality that all readers can share in, and the scenes of more conventional adventures – witnessing the murder in the cemetery, hiding in the haunted house, being lost in the darkness of the cave – are exciting and suspenseful. But much of the time young readers have simply to ignore the novel's third person narrator, who maintains several different kinds of distance from the lives of the book's child characters. There is the distance of tone: although sympathetic to the hopes and fears of the children he is writing about, he often invites us to be amused by the things they take seriously – the whole courtship of Tom and Becky, for instance, is played for laughs. There is also the distance of perspective: the narrator has lived a longer, larger life, and can continuously make comparisons from the vantage point of his matured experience. When Tom masters a new way to whistle, we're told, "He felt much as an astronomer feels who has discovered a new planet. No doubt, as far as strong, deep, unalloyed pleasure is concerned, the advantage was with the boy, not the astronomer" (5).

"The advantage was with the boy" – this is the belief that sustains the novel, the fiction of childhood as a kind of golden age. Even the cares of children are like the "money" Tom's pockets are stuffed with: really trifles. This is not the way childhood is lived – to children there is nothing funny about their hopes and fears – but it is often remembered that way by the same adults who, paradoxically, once were so impatient to grow up. The distance that makes the world of *Tom*

Sawyer so delectable can be summed up with one word: nostalgia. The novel's deepest pleasures are most accessible to older readers, for whom playing with Tom offers a respite from such intractable adult realities as work, money and death. Children constantly make plans for and rehearse their adulthood. Hymns to childhood are created by adults who have "reached middle age with unsatisfied ambition" – or who realize that fulfilling their ambitions still leaves them unsatisfied. This seems to have been Twain's case. According to the record he left of his life, the first time he imaginatively went back to Hannibal was in 1870. Just four days after marrying Livy and moving into the fine house paid for by his father-in-law, he wrote an extraordinary letter to Will Bowen, the real childhood friend on whom Joe Harper's character is based, in reply to a letter Will had written him. The verbal picture he draws for Will of the genteel life he and Livy now enjoy in "the daintiest, darlingest, loveliest little palace in America" is not unlike the image Tom draws on his slate for Becky, but the most enthusiastic part of Twain's letter describes the memories that Will's name has conjured up. "I have rained reminiscences for four & twenty hours," he writes, and goes on for over 500 words to eloquently recall the lives they shared 25 years earlier – playing "Robin Hood in our shirt-tales . . . in the woods on Holliday's Hill," "swimming above the still-house branch," and so on.[8] Four years later, as he and Livy were setting up as the master and mistress of a considerably larger "palace," that childhood world took possession of his imagination again. As Twain knew, he wrote *Tom Sawyer* for adults like himself: the novel does not so much recover the past as create a myth of childhood in which readers, older readers especially, can recover a redemptive idea of the possibilities of life as an adventure.

Similar to the recuperative role the story can play for individual readers is the demonstrable cultural value that *The Adventures of Tom Sawyer* has had for generations of Americans. Nostalgia is a temptation that societies as well as adults can succumb to, and in the last quarter of the 19th century American society was coming of age in ways that made its earlier life very attractive. After the Civil War the nation went through exactly the kinds of cultural dislocations and ruptures that endow the idea of a simpler, safer past with great ideological power. The abstract terms for the most important of these changes are urbanization, industrialization and immigration. In 1860, for example, on the same chronological side of the Civil War that the novel is set in, fewer than one in five Americans lived in cities; by 1890, over one-third of the population did. At the time *Tom Sawyer* takes place – circa 1845 – manufacturing was already the fastest growing segment of the economy, but the national self-image was still essentially agricultural; by the beginning of the 20th century, however, about one-quarter of all jobs were in factories; by 1920, that percentage would rise to about one-half, and, given the novel's emphasis on children playing, it is worth remembering that in the real United States child industrial labor was not outlawed until the 1930s. The ethnic face of the population changed dramatically during this period too. The waves of immigration did not peak until 1907, when 1.2 million people came to the United States from abroad, but the impact of cultural diversity (to use a non-pejorative term for what, to many older Americans, seemed like an invasion of alien languages, belief systems, traditions and so on) was felt much earlier. In her autobiography, Jane Addams, who grew up in an Illinois village less than 200 miles from Hannibal, provides a powerful image of the new America that Twain was writing for in her description of Halstead Street in Chicago in 1889:

> Polk Street crosses it midway between the stockyards to the south and the shipbuilding yards on the north branch of the Chicago River. For the six miles between these two industries the street is lined with shops of butchers and grocers, with dingy and gorgeous saloons, and pretentious establishments for the sale of ready-made clothing . . . Between Halstead Street and the river live about ten thousand Italians . . . To the south on Twelfth Street are many Germans, and side streets are given over almost entirely to Polish and Russian Jews. Still farther south, these Jewish colonies merge into a huge Bohemian colony, so vast that Chicago ranks as the third Bohemian city in the world.[9]

As an urban reformer, Jane Addams tackled the challenges of this new America directly. For writers like Stephen Crane and Theodore Dreiser, the industrialized city was a metaphorically perfect setting for their proto-modernist novels of alienation and insignificance. Middle-class Americans, however, generally preferred to escape rather than confront the cultural disruptions of the *fin de siècle*, which explains why the period's most popular literary mode was the form of regionalist fiction called "local color." If you browse the pages of mass-market magazines like *Scribner's* or *The Century* from the last decades of the 19th century, you are almost certain to find short stories set in rural or small town environments: California mining camps (cf. Bret Harte) or New England villages (cf. Harriet Beecher Stowe, Mary E. Wilkins Freeman or Sarah Orne Jewett) or the bayous of Creole Louisiana (cf. Kate Chopin) and so on. St Petersburg is a similarly pastoral setting. Twain's novel gives American readers another form of transport back to a world that can be described with phrases like "those easy times" (30) and "those old simple days" (255), remote from the many cultural complexities of modernity. The census of the characters' Anglo-Saxon last names – Sawyer, Harper, Thatcher, Douglas – suggests how essentially homogenous is the village's population: they all attend the same church, for example, and when a "Spaniard" apparently does migrate into the community he turns out really to be the narrative's all-purpose outsider, "Injun Joe," in disguise.

Of course, the population isn't really homogenous: like Hannibal, St Petersburg is a slave-owning society. One of the most popular strains of local color fiction took the form of "plantation tales." These were written by southern writers like Joel Chandler Harris and Thomas Nelson Page, but were equally popular with northern readers. Stories in this genre began appearing in the 1880s. Whether *Tom Sawyer* should be considered an early example of the genre is an intriguing question. The explicit goal of Page's stories in a best-selling collection like *In Ole Virginia* (1887) is to enshrine the ante bellum plantation as an American Camelot, and to celebrate the institution of slavery as the ideal relationship between whites and blacks. The racial politics of *Tom Sawyer* are not nearly so transparent. The word "slave" hardly appears in the text: Jim, for instance, the one slave Aunt Polly owns, is referred to simply as "the small colored boy" (3). After Mary scrubs the dirt off Tom's face in preparation for Sunday School, the narrator describes him as "a man and a brother, without distinction of color" (28), turning the slogan of the Anti-Slavery Society and the larger question of racial equality into the occasion for a joke. When Tom thinks about the "company" he might find hanging about the town pump, the text refers to "white, mulatto and negro boys and girls" (11) – out of the charged interracial relationships this list implies would come the ironies of *Pudd'nhead Wilson*, but the phrase gives *Tom Sawyer*'s reader no reason to pause. In Twain's subsequent books about the landscape of his childhood, *Huckleberry Finn* and *Pudd'nhead Wilson*, slavery occupies an increasingly important place in the story.

In *Tom Sawyer* the existence of slavery in the paradise of St Petersburg is simultaneously evoked and dismissed, acknowledged but emptied of any moral or social significance.

Twain performs the same act of erasure in the other autobiographical text he wrote in 1874–5, the year during which *Tom Sawyer* was composed. This was the series of articles about his apprenticeship as a cub steamboat pilot, published as "Old Times on the Mississippi" in *The Atlantic* magazine in seven monthly installments, then re-used as the opening section of his travel book *Life on the Mississippi* (1883). Like *Tom Sawyer*, "Old Times" is an act of invention rather than memory, a masterful piece of story telling rather than a faithful account of real experience. It is also among Twain's most enjoyable works. In it he casts himself, as "the cub," in the same role he had played in his earlier first-person travel books: he is the hapless naif, the innocent whose inevitable incompetence provides repeated opportunities for comedy. At the same time he casts "Mr. B—," his teacher, as a "lightning pilot" whose feats of skill and courage resemble the outsized actions of legendary tall-tale heroes like Davy Crockett or Mike Fink. Between looking down on and laughing at the Cub and looking up to and admiring the Pilot, the reader is thoroughly entertained. These sketches established the relationship between "Mark Twain" and the Mississippi riverboat that have been so much a part of his image as an American celebrity, a kind of tall-tale hero himself. But in the way they mythologize those "old times," they filter out most of the picture. Although Twain devotes an installment, for example, to the issue of the pilots' salaries, the larger economic realities that created the thriving river traffic in the late 1850s, the markets for cotton and slaves, are not mentioned. (The one time a boat he is on lands a slave owner at his plantation, it is too dark to see either the slave who awaits him or the plantation.) Similarly the fact that most crew members on most boats were African Americans, including many who were enslaved, is acknowledged so surreptitiously that most of the sketches' readers at the time, and most of Twain's readers still, do not appreciate that the leadsmen's voices that called out "mark twain" whenever soundings were taken were almost always *black* voices.

"Old Times" begins with the talismanic words "When I was a boy . . ." and locates the story it is telling in the same setting as *Tom Sawyer*: "After all these years I can picture that old time to myself now, just as it was then: the white town drowsing in the sunshine of a summer's morning . . ."[10] The first voice we hear actually belongs to a slave: "a negro drayman, famous for his quick eye and prodigious voice, lifts up the cry, 'S-t-e-a-m-boat a-comin'!'" But from that point on, as in *Tom Sawyer*, the African Americans whose labor gave the steamboat its power and the "white town" its prosperity are essentially silent and invisible. In these texts Twain gives American culture access to an idea of the past that is in its own way as restorative as the novel's fantasy of childhood. It is a past where playing [white] boys skinny-dip in a mighty river on which working [white] men perform feats of greatness, where a whole village rejoices and sorrows together over the fortunes and misfortunes of its [white] children. Set right in the middle of the continent, it is an idea of the past to which the nation continues to go gratefully, as a means of anchoring our self-image to a fixed point in a world that, like a river, keeps flowing and changing. It is not clear that as many children read *Tom Sawyer* now as did for most of the 20th century, but film versions of the story continue to replay its images of that reassuring ante bellum past. In order to meet the needs of nostalgia, however, that past must be drastically white-washed, most of its complexities kept out of sight. "Society in the Mississippi Valley in Tom Sawyer's time," according to an appreciation of Twain written in 1907, "was a pure democracy, in easy circumstances, free from anxiety, charitable of everything except cowardice and meanness, taking life comfortably." According to such grateful readers, this is not myth-making but history, and Twain is not the creator of "this old-time life," but rather "the interpreter and recorder."[11] Twain himself, on the other hand, seems to have realized that *Tom Sawyer* obscures as much as it reveals about that past, for he kept going back to take different, less nostalgic looks at it in later books, as we will see in later chapters.

A fast-paced series of wonderful adventures, a vacation from adulthood and an unfading vision of an idyllic past – these are the main wishes that the novel fulfills for its readers. For Twain himself, writing *Tom Sawyer* also provided a chance to address a concern that had, after ten years of being "Mark Twain," begun to haunt him, a question about the implications of his public success that would grow more urgent throughout the rest of his career. Explaining that will give us a chance to look a bit more closely at the story's hero. Tom Sawyer is of course one of the best-known characters in American literature. Based on his reputation, it seems that the trait most people recognize him by is his truant disposition, the high-spirited love of adventure that makes him so restless with the disciplines of civilization that aunts and teachers and other grown-ups keep trying to impose on him. Tom does misbehave a lot, playing hookey from school, sneaking out at night, running away to Jackson's Island, eating the forbidden jam. But much of the time even his mischievous acts are part of his larger need for attention. The most fundamental fact of Tom's personality is that he is a compulsive performer. "The looks" and "the remarks" of others, the narrator admits at one point, are "food and drink" to Tom (137); his deepest quest is not for freedom from restraint, but for what the novel refers to as "dazzling notoriety" (111), "glittering notoreity" (137), "glittering hero[ism]" (173). And the novel shares his obsessive concern with performance. Its opening scene, for example, is not just a re-writing of the book of Genesis; it is also staged as a complete theatrical performance in miniature. It begins with Aunt Polly introducing or calling for the star of the show: "TOM!" is the book's first word, and it is repeated twice more while the star keeps the audience waiting long enough to arouse expectations. He comes onstage, has a short comic dialogue with Polly, improvises a very dramatic exit line, then goes offstage by disappearing behind the fence, leaving Polly behind to laugh at the joke he has played and even to offer a brief review of his performance that emphasizes Tom's ability to manipulate and entertain his audience: "'He 'pears to know just how long he can torment me before I get my dander up, and he knows if he can make out to put me off for a minute or make me laugh, it's all down again and I can't hit him a lick'" (1–3).

Many of the novel's most elaborate scenes are similarly scenes of performance. Tom even treats running away as a kind of show that should be advertised ahead of time: before he, Joe and Huck light out for the island, "they had all managed to enjoy the sweet glory of spreading the fact that pretty soon the town would 'hear something'" (99). And the way they return from the island turns their running away into a kind of stage wait, in which Tom keeps the boys offstage until they can make the most dramatic entrance possible. By reappearing in church at his own funeral, Tom not only triumphs over death, but at the same time turns the mournful villagers into "the house" for whom he is putting on a show. The church becomes a kind of theater, in which Tom's clever stage managing gives the villagers the most deeply moving experience they have ever had in church, even though it is a theatrical illusion: the "funeral" climaxes with a song, and "As the 'sold' congregation trooped out they said they would almost be willing to be made ridiculous again to hear Old Hundred sung like that once more" (131–2). Several Sundays previously Tom had also helped to entertain the congregation when he accidentally dropped a pinch-bug during the service; "uninterested in the sermon," the people were delighted with the slightly off-color comedy provided by the bug and a poodle that wanders into church (42). Give us this day our daily entertainment – this seems to be the motto of the villagers. Tom is always willing to oblige.

"Pretty soon the town will hear something" closely resembles the advertising "Mark Twain" did whenever he went town to town on his lecture tours. The novel's thematic preoccupation with performance is as autobiographical as its setting in a village beside the river. As in all his public work, Twain is writing the novel *as* a performance, but at the same time, because it is a novel, because he can project his compulsion to perform onto a created character, he can also use the story to interrogate the process of defining a self through performing for others. At first. it seems as if he is determined to look more critically at that process than at anything else in this otherwise nostalgically indulgent narrative. Tom's resurrection at his own funeral is such a great piece of showmanship that we may be tempted to overlook how its effect depends on coldly manipulating the real feelings of "the house," but there is nothing theatrical about Aunt Polly or Mrs. Harper's grief. In the way the congregation is "sold" in this scene Twain acknowledges some of what it costs, in human terms, to turn life into a show. The novel's first scene of public performance makes this process still more problematic.

That scene also has an eccelesiastical context. The Sunday after the white-washing episode Tom decides to swap his newly gained wealth for the other boys' Sunday School chits. The value of these tickets is supposed to be tied to learning the Bible; any child who has learned two thousand verses can trade them in for a new Bible and, more importantly, for the prestige of being "so great and conspicuous" (31) as a successful scholar. Tom, though able to recite pages from adventure stories like Robin Hood, has trouble memorizing even the shortest scriptural passages, and has no interest whatever in the Bible, "but unquestionably," the narrator writes, "his entire being had for many a day longed for the glory and the eclat that came with it" (31). That is the set up to the scene in which Tom takes center stage in Sunday School, and "therefore elevate[s] himself to a place with . . . the elect," by presenting an astonished Superintendent with the requisite number of tickets and claiming the reward (34). Although played as comedy, the scene raises several serious questions. In the world of *Tom Sawyer*, even in church the "elect" are not the souls whom God has saved, but people with public status. By gaining all that attention, Tom makes himself a "hero" – that is actually the word that the narrative uses – even though he is also "a wily fraud" (34). In fact, before the end of the episode the glittering hero will be exposed as a gilded impostor, a false claimant. Twain will write such scenes of exposure – in which, for example, the prince turns out to be a pauper, or a king and a duke a pair of conmen, or a bag of gold coins a sack of worthless lead – repeatedly throughout his career. That he treats Tom Sawyer's very first public triumph as such a sham suggests his own misgivings, from behind the curtain of his own triumphant career as "Mark Twain," about looking for salvation in an audience's eyes. And Tom not only abuses others in this scene; there is the additional question of the way he is betraying himself. Although we're told "his entire being" longs to shine as a Sunday School hero, the narrator also says, a few pages earlier, that Sunday School was "a place that Tom hated with his whole heart" (29). That his "whole heart" and his "entire being" are so completely split, that he needs the applause of a group he despises, suggests how anxiously Twain is using Tom to dramatize the dangers of defining one's life as a performance: to satisfy the appetites of his audience, Tom has to deny the truth about himself.

As the novel goes on, however, Twain casts Tom's actions in a much more reassuring light. After the Sunday School and funeral scenes, Tom's next major public performance occurs at Muff Potter's trial. Once again a social institution, in this case a legal proceding in a courtroom, is turned into a kind of theater where Tom can claim center stage: as he describes what he saw that night in the cemetery, "every sound ceased but his own voice; every eye fixed itself upon him; with parted lips and bated breath the audience hung upon his words" (172). Although Tom's testimony elevates him again to the status of "glittering hero" (173), this time he is no fraud. In fact, by testifying Tom is serving justice: he establishes Muff's innocence and fixes the guilt where it truly belongs, on "Injun Joe." Tom's final act

of heroism goes even further to recuperate his credentials as a legit-
imate hero. After he and Becky have been lost in the cave for just
about the same amount of time as he, Joe and Huck had spent on
Jackson's Island, and the townspeople have once again given up hope,
he manages another return from the dead, saving himself and the
heroine by finding a way back to the sunlight. This time no make-
believe or manipulation is involved. Indeed, this act of heroism is
performed *in the dark*, where no one else can see it. The real victory
parade that St Petersburg spontaneously creates for the saved children
is a kind of redemptive antithesis to the sham funeral service earlier:
"The village was illuminated; nobody went to bed again; it was the
greatest night the little town had ever seen" (234). Tom's compulsion
to shine in others' eyes has not abated, as we see in the last "specta-
cle" he enacts (252): when he pours out the treasure he and Huck
have recovered from the cave to steal the show the Welshman and
the Widow have arranged for Huck, we may be reminded of the
spendthrift way Tom was prepared to exchange his wealth for attention in Sunday School (or, for that matter, of the way Twain was
pouring money into his trophy Hartford house). But unlike Tom's
claims as a Bible scholar, this time what glitters is real gold. By the
end, when the narrator tells us that Tom is "courted, admired, stared
at" (254), the narrative has taken all taint of fraud or bad faith away
from his "notoreity."

Yet while Twain and his readers have many good reasons to savor
Tom's success as both a glittering and a 24-karat hero, both a schem-
ing supplicant for popular favor and a genuinely good kid, the novel
gives us one compelling reason to doubt that Twain himself was able
completely to resolve all his anxieties about being somebody through
publically enacting a self. That reason is named Huckleberry Finn. To
students of Twain's career, indeed, to students of American literature,
one of the great fascinations in reading *Tom Sawyer* is watching Huck's
place in the narrative grow, until by the end, despite all Tom's gifts as
a performer, Huck is threatening to steal the show away from him.
Huck is introduced in chapter 6 as the "son of the town drunkard,"
the "juvenile pariah of the village" with whom the "respectable boys"
have been forbidden to associate (47). He and Tom make plans to go
to the graveyard that midnight, which they do in chapters 9–10.
When Tom and Joe Harper decide to run away in chapter 13, they
ask Huck to come along, which brings Huck back into Tom's story

during the next four chapters. The novel, however, is still very much Tom's story: when his conscience drives Tom to testify on Muff Potter's behalf in chapter 23, Huck remains offstage even though he could corroborate Tom's evidence. But soon afterwards, from chapter 25 onward, Huck becomes the novel's other main character when Tom asks him to join in the search for buried treasure. According to the narrator, Tom asks Huck because he "failed to find Joe Harper" (175), but it is also clear that Twain's imagination has become inspired by the possibilities in Huck's character. After chapter 25 Joe disappears and Huck is almost continuously onstage. The exception occurs when Tom goes off to Becky's picnic and the adventure of the cave, but at that point the novel does something that few readers could have anticipated: divides its focus between what Tom is doing with Becky and what Huck is doing by himself (the narrative assumes Huck's point-of-view in chapters 29–30). By the logic of the story Twain was writing at the start of the novel – a gentle burlesque of adult romance, in which the hero and heroine marry at the end – the book's concluding chapter should have featured Tom with Becky. Instead, as final proof of how strongly Twain's interest has shifted from Tom to Huck, the last chapter of *Tom Sawyer* revolves around the question of Huck's future, as Tom convinces him to live with the widow and become "respectable" enough to join the robber gang that Tom is planning to form. It is Huck who gets the book's last spoken words.

Huck himself would not have appreciated the increasing attention that the novel pays to him. Huck, in fact, hates attention. That is the most conspicuous difference between his character and Tom's. Tom lives to see himself reflected in other people's eyes; his happiest moments are when the attention of a crowd is fastened on him. Huck, on the other hand, is "abashed and uncomfortable" as one of the stars of the funeral service, and "the loving attention Aunt Polly lavishe[s] upon him" at that event makes him "more uncomfortable than he was before" (131). His impulse at such moments is to hide, to "slink away" (131), or, as he puts it to Tom when he feels trapped by an attentive audience again at the end, to "slope" (250). Tom cannot begin to understand why Huck would want to abandon center stage, but as Huck tells him: "Well I ain't used to that kind of a crowd. I can't stand it" (250). Writing about Tom gave Twain an imaginative means to renew the shine on the prize of popular notoriety that had been the object of his quest at least since becoming a writer, but Huck's character offered a chance to step almost completely outside the dynamic of defining a self by performance. Given his misgivings about that process, it is perhaps not surprising that even before *Tom Sawyer* was published in the United States, Mark Twain was hard at work writing a new novel – as Huck Finn.

Running Away
Adventures of Huckleberry Finn

"All modern American literature," according to Ernest Hemingway's most famous overstatement, "comes from one book by Mark Twain called 'Huckleberry Finn.'"[1] And what about postmodern literature? Has Mark Twain ever gotten the credit he deserves for being the first novelist to take a character from the margins of one classic novel and put that character at the center of a new, revisionary fiction? This strategy is usually traced back to Jean Rhys' *Wide Sargasso Sea* (1966), a first-person narrative written from the perspective of Rochester's first wife, the mysterious foreign madwoman in the attic of Charlotte Bronte's *Jane Eyre* (1847). Future literary historians will surely include such intertextual transformations as a defining trait of fiction from the last third of the twentieth century: *Robinson Crusoe, Moby-Dick*, even *Gone With the Wind* are among the many classic novels that have been retold from a radically different point of view. But almost 100 years earlier Twain is doing much the same thing in *Adventures of Huckleberry Finn* (1885), his re-writing of *The Adventures of Tom Sawyer*[2] from Huck's first-person perspective. Of course, *Tom Sawyer* had not yet become a classic when, in 1876, Twain began writing *Huck Finn*; in fact, it had not even been published yet in the United States. And unlike contemporary revisionists, Twain is re-writing a novel that he wrote himself. But *Huck Finn* is almost as radical a re-envisioning as any postmodern sensibility could imagine.

We shouldn't overstate Twain's modernity, however. He had his own reasons for deciding to take another imaginative look, this time through Huck's eyes, at the world he had grown up in. Typically, the characters on whom postmodern novelists are most likely to hang a new version of an older tale are figures who, in the originating text, have been marginalized on account of their race, gender or class. Huck certainly qualifies on the grounds of class: as the "poor white" son of the town drunk, he is introduced in *Tom Sawyer* as an "outcast" who is kept at a distance from the village's "respectable boys."[3] But while Twain uses Huck's class status to explore aspects of village life that *Tom Sawyer* excluded – specifically, life with Pap – the part of Huck's character that he found most useful is his illiteracy. This certainly derives from his social class (neither his mother nor father, nor "none of the family" could read or write[4]), but the uses to which Twain puts it are part of his project as a 19th-century realist writer. The fact that Huck is not a reader is what allows him to be so powerful a writer – or, to use the term we introduced in chapter 1, what enables him to write one of the greatest classics of American literature by *un*-writing another.

Twain's never gotten enough credit for the brilliant first sentence of *Huck Finn* either, though if I italicize its last five words it should be easier to appreciate its revisionary power: "You don't know about me without you have read a book by the name of 'The Adventures of Tom Sawyer,' *but that ain't no matter*" (1). Huck goes on to give *Tom Sawyer* his qualified endorsement: it's "mostly a true book," he says, but notes twice in that first paragraph that it contains "some stretchers." In those last five words, however, he puts a great distance between himself and "Mr. Mark Twain," the man who "made" *Tom Sawyer*. Twain actually added those last five words in a revision to the manuscript[5]; given his own stake, financial and otherwise, in having people buy and read the prequel to Huck's book, he is doing a remarkable thing when he allows Huck to dismiss *Tom Sawyer* so completely. Although we must not ask how Huck in the 1850s could possibly have read a book that Twain wrote and published in the 1870s, it is with this gesture that Huck defines himself, and not only against Twain as a maker of books but also against nearly everyone else in the story as readers of books.

To them, reading books matters a lot. Huck has to fend off a number of other books during his novel's opening chapters. On page 2, the Widow gets out "her book" – as Huck calls the Bible that the Widow herself would probably call The Book – and forces Huck to listen to the story of Moses on the Nile, even though Huck himself "don't take no stock in dead people." On page 3, Miss Watson "[takes] a set at

[him] now, with a spelling-book." Even when Tom summons him out of the house in the middle of the night for what should be play, Huck is still confronted with books, in this case the "pirate books and robber books" that Tom uses to organize his friends into a robber gang. The Widow, Miss Watson and Tom are not re-writers, but very literal, deferential readers. Miss Watson, for example, takes Huck "in the closet" to pray (12) because of what is written in the New Testament (Matthew 6:6), just as Tom insists the gang has to "ransom" the prisoners it takes, even though none of the boys know what "ransom" means – "I've seen it in books;" Tom says, "and so of course that's what we've got to do" (10). In these opening scenes Tom, the tentative "outsider" of *Tom Sawyer*, is being realigned with the feminine guardians of conventionality who had seemed his antagonists, at least on the ground of their similar devotion to books as scriptures. As a result of his virtual illiteracy, Huck becomes the new novel's point of opposition to all this bookishness. Chapter 3 fully establishes Huck's difference from the other characters and their various textual authorities. It begins with Huck praying for fishhooks to test what Miss Watson has told him about the God of the Bible, and ends with Huck rubbing an old lamp to test Tom's statements about the genies of *The Arabian Nights*. These subtly paired incidents not only align Christianity with romances as imaginative constructs – both the Bible and *The Arabian Nights*, we may realize with a shock, are collections of stories from the Middle East that Americans read in imported translations. Huck's experimentations here also reveal that he has a basis for knowing that is not dependent on reading: the basis of his own personal experience. This unmediated contact with reality is what provides him with a position from which to resist the texts the other characters revere so uncritically, and to rewrite the book that was made by "Mr. Mark Twain."

To some extent, Mr. Twain has already made us very familiar with much of what he is now using Huck to do. In chapter 12, for instance, when Huck and Jim go on board the wrecked steamboat *Walter Scott*, the real robber gang they run into is nothing like gang Tom organizes in chapter 2, which he models on the idealized, picturesque brigands and buccaneers that he reads about in romances by writers like Walter Scott. In Tom's mind robbers are chivalrous and brave; in Huck's actual experience they are mean cowards who stink of whisky. This is the rhythm of realist novels as a genre, the fall from romantic fancies to stark actualities; it is also the rhythm of Twain's travel books, where the occasion for disillusionment can be the gap between Cooper's "Noble Red Man" and the unpicturesque Goshoot Indians Twain encounters in the real West of *Roughing It*. When Huck translates Emmeline Grangerford's cliche-ridden and sentimental "Ode to Stephen Dowling Bots" into his own straightforward report – it was "about a boy . . . that fell down a well and was drownded" (139), or tells us that *Pilgrim's Progress* is a book "about a man that left his family it didn't say why" (137), Huck's naive allegiance to what he can see with his own eyes and his equally revelatory ability *not* to see what *isn't* there give Twain a very sharp tool with which to keep exposing the experiential emptiness behind so much of what one finds in books. As we noted earlier, this is a fundamental theme in *Innocents Abroad*, where the opposition between Tom and Huck – between, that is, books and experience – is repeatedly dramatized as the conflict between the ideal world described in the guide books to Europe and the Holy Land and the material world Twain's senses perceive. The signature line of *Innocents* – "Is he dead?" – anticipates Huck's refusal to take stock in dead people, just as *Huck Finn* too is the narrative of a journey, by raft instead of steamship. Yet the "holy land" that is being deconstructed in *Huck Finn* is much closer to home for both Twain and his readers: "St Petersburg" as a heavenly realm, a beautiful vision of Twain's own and America's past. In the opening of his narrative, Huck is quietly telling us that he will be revising the received account of his own creation.

One other question we must not ask is how Huck, who as late as chapter 2 of *Huck Finn* cannot even sign his own name (cf. 10), could write a novel at all. To resolve this implausibility, some commentators have suggested that his story should be read essentially as an oral narrative. Huck's voice is vividly conversational, but he himself refers at the end to what he has been doing as "mak[ing] a book," as "writ[ing]" not talking (362). The main point, however, is that Huck cannot make a conventional book, just as he cannot, despite his sincere efforts, write a sentimental poem for Emmeline: "I tried to sweat out a verse or two myself, but I couldn't seem to make it go, somehow" (141). His failure here as a poet explains the vivifying achievement of the prose in which *Huck Finn* is written, the revolutionary significance of Huck's voice as the style of the novel. Emmeline's poetry is made of words like "list" (for "listen"), words, that is, that are exactly like the stanzaic structure of her "Ode" and like its description of the fate of the dead boy's soul: "His spirit was gone for to sport aloft/In the realms of the good and great" (139). All three of these features – diction, form, theme – come from the books Emmeline has read, not the real life she has lived. Just as she has never actually *seen* those realms "aloft" where Stephen attains his heavenly reward, so she has never *heard* anyone say "list." Huck cannot write poetry like Emmeline's because he hasn't read the texts that authorize her text. Tom, on the other hand, could write such a poem, as proved by the "mournful inscriptions" he ghost-writes for Jim, with such phrases as "a worn spirit went to its rest" (322); Tom's sentimental prose and Emmeline's poetry imitate somewhat different texts, but what's strikingly similar is the way these two middle American children, both about Huck's age, already define "reality" and their own voices according to linguistic and ideological conventions they know only through European books.

Tom repeatedly gets annoyed with Huck's cultural illiteracy, telling him at one point that he should have "read a book called 'Don Quixote'" (15) and angrily complaining at another: "Huck, you don't ever seem to want to do anything that's regular: you want to be starting something fresh all the time" (300–1). What exasperates Tom, however, inspires Twain. Aesthetically, Huck's ignorance of literary discourse means that Twain can use him to recreate American life in its own idioms, not those derived from imported texts. Huck is free and unselfconscious about using his own voice in ways that even "Mark Twain" could not be, for Twain knew that his rhetorical success depended on keeping his prose in a vaguely marked channel between the vernacular on one side and the literary on the other. From American slang his voice acquired the naughtiness and force that made listening to him so entertaining. However, from regular retreats into standard forms of genteel elegance – the "poetic" descriptive passages in his travel books, for example – Twain not only reassured his audience that he spoke their language and thus was one of them, but also enabled them to enjoy the subversive energy of the vernacular without feeling threatened by it. In *Tom Sawyer* and *Huck Finn* there are several places where "Mark Twain" and Huck both describe the same things. To compare such passages is to hear how conventional Twain's idiom can be, and how immediate, how unmediated by linguistic conventions, how vivid and subversive is Huck's.

For one brief example, we can listen to each narrator describing the thunder during two storms on Jackson's Island (chapter 16 of *Tom Sawyer*, chapter 9 of *Huck Finn*). "But at last the battle was done, and the forces retired with weaker and weaker threatenings and grumblings, and peace resumed her sway." "And now you'd hear the thunder let go with an awful crash and then go rumbling, grumbling, tumbling down the sky towards the under side of the world, like rolling empty barrels down stairs, where it's long stairs and they bounce a good deal, you know" (59–60). It is easy to tell which is Huck's voice. He doesn't know how to mount a sustained simile (storm as warfare) or how to personify abstractions (peace). He has never witnessed a battle, though he has heard both thunder and barrels rolling down stairs. Of course, neither Twain nor most of his readers have ever witnessed a battle either, but from the other books they have read they know that thunderstorms are supposed to sound like battles and so, by the illogic of convention, what they have never experienced can be used to express what they already know firsthand. In a sense, the *Tom Sawyer* passage gives readers shelter from the storm itself, by converting it into a well-known metaphor. Huck's voice, on the other hand, keeps us in contact with the world he lives in. Huck likes to sleep in empty barrels, and as the son of the town drunk he would have seen a lot of them. The way his figures of speech arise out of his own experience is the stylistic equivalent to testing what Tom tells him about genies with his own lamp: he knows *and says* what he sees for himself. There are many passages in *Huck Finn* that radiate with Twain's excitement at having found in Huck's vernacular a means of taking direct linguistic possession of reality: descriptions of the river at night or in the fog, or of the sunrise, or of the Grangerfords' parlor, and so on. Almost certainly it was the novel's style, the way Huck's voice gave subsequent writers a model for making literature out of American experience rather than European books, that Hemingway was thinking of when he credited the book with inaugurating a "modern" aesthetic.

Autobiographically, revisiting Hannibal as St Petersburg from Huck's point of view means that Twain can get much closer to the look and feel of the world he grew up in than he could in *Tom Sawyer*. Seen through Huck's eyes that world no longer looks like the "Delectable Land, dreamy, reposeful and inviting."[6] Indeed, the more you see through Huck's eyes, the more you can appreciate the fact that the most memorable scene in *Tom Sawyer* is a white-washing. In it, for example, the sources of fear and evil are mainly projected onto the melodramatic figure of "Injun Joe," racially and socially an "Other" despised by decent society. At the beginning of *Huck Finn*, Pap seems cast to play a similar role, and in his case caste could serve as race does with Joe to segregate the villain from the respectable people either in St Petersburg or in Twain's reading public. But Pap disappears very quickly from the narrative, which turns its attention instead to "decent" society – the quotation marks here are made necessary by what Huck encounters in that world. He spends two chapters, for example, among the Grangerfords, "quality folk" who wear suits "so white [they] hurt your eyes to look at" and kill children in the name of honor (142). When a bit later the respectable people of Bricksville are aroused by an act of violence and transformed into a lynch mob, Huck's metaphor indicates how completely the lines that might have shielded white society from being recognized as a source of horror have been erased: "They swarmed up the street . . . yelling and raging like Injuns" (189).

"It was awful to see," Huck adds, in a phrase that becomes a kind of refrain in the book: "I wished I hadn't ever come ashore," he says at another point, "to see such things" (153); "It was a dreadful thing to see," he says after another scene of cruelty and violence (290). In *Tom Sawyer* St Petersburg is depicted nostalgically, as the place we long to return to. *Huck Finn*, however, is anti-nostalgic: the story is about running away from St Petersburg. Return would mean defeat. Huck is not consciously a social critic. In fact, he believes in the moral superiority of "aristocracy" like the Shepherdsons and Grangerfords. His own visceral reactions, however, testify to the moral uninhabitability of the social status quo. Huck has to keep moving, because in all the places he goes ashore the human landscape is dominated by forms of bigotry, hypocrisy, greed, cowardice and brutality. Of course, Huck doesn't use abstract terms like brutality, but his prose remains in contact with what his experience reveals, and there is a lot in this white world that hurts your eyes to look at.

The most significant difference between the representation of the ante bellum past in *Tom Sawyer* and in *Huck Finn* involves the depiction of slavery. Twain's re-use of the name Jim may have been meant to signal this revision. In *Tom Sawyer*, Jim is the slave whom Aunt Polly owns, although the narrator avoids the term slave by identifying him as "the small colored boy."[7] In *Huck Finn*, Jim is the name of Miss Watson's slave, not a small boy but a big man. His much larger place in the narrative is indicated by the fact that the very first line of dialogue in the novel, the first voice we hear besides Huck's, belongs to Jim: "Who dah?" (6) When it turns out in chapter 8 that Jim himself is "there" on Jackson's Island, the novel makes slavery the occasion for its own narrative. From the moment that Huck, running away from Pap and the Widow, agrees to help Jim run away from Miss Watson, the story is organized as a quest for freedom.

But while the problem of slavery, which had been invisible in *Tom Sawyer*, is central to *Huck Finn*, Twain is not primarily interested in what the institution of slavery was like for slaves, but in what it means, ideologically, to society as a whole, and in how it can be used, metaphorically, to explore the way ideology itself operates on human consciousness. Can Huck help free Jim? That is the question on which the plot will essentially turn as the two runaways travel downriver on the raft. But hidden in that is the novel's deepest thematic question: can Jim help free Huck? Huck raises the issue of his freedom on the novel's very first page: "[I] was free and satisfied" is how he describes himself after he has "lit out" from the Widow's attempts to "sivilize" him and gone back to sleeping in an empty barrel. Freedom for Huck thus starts off as a visceral condition: freedom from the constrictions and frustrations of genteel respectability. After Pap kidnaps him, his confinement becomes much more severe, and his captivity more analogous to Jim's enslavement. Pap holds Huck hostage for the sake of $6,000, just as Miss Watson thinks about selling Jim for $800; in both cases, people are being commodified. Freedom for Huck, though, is still a physical matter: to free himself from Pap he need only go as far as Jackson's Island, which is originally as far as he plans to go. But when Twain puts Jim on the island too, the whole matter of Huck's freedom is reconceptualized. He must now struggle with the contradiction between Jim's claims on him as a friend and fellow human being, and the cultural conditioning that has taught him to see African Americans as "niggers," to believe that slavery is right, and to look upon helping a fugitive slave escape as the wickedest possible way to transgress the commandment against stealing.[8] By redefining Huck's "enslavement" in this way, as ideological, the novel removes the ground of his possible freedom to a very different place than Jackson's Island, or even the "free states" that would constitute Jim's freedom from Miss Watson. Freedom for Huck becomes an intellectual condition: it depends on reaching a conclusion rather than a place, on attaining an insight into the inadequacy of his culture's values and arriving at a belief in the value, even the superior authority of his own personal convictions.

We must, therefore, qualify our notion of Huck's illiteracy. He has not read books, but one of the most illuminating points *Huck Finn* dramatizes is how cultures define themselves and "reality" by unwritten as well as written "texts." One such unwritten text is the "saying" that Huck quotes in chapter 16, as he grows increasingly uncomfortable listening to Jim talk about what he'll do once he is free: "It was according to the old saying, 'give a nigger an inch and he'll take an ell'" (124). To Huck, that kind of "saying" has the same scriptural authority as the codes Tom and the Widow find in their books, and the same power to create "reality." Although no one is there to say it to Huck, that old "saying" speaks louder than anything Jim can say. While Jim is talking as a husband and father about his desire to be united with his family in freedom, what Huck hears is what he refers to later as "an ungrateful nigger" (268) – "ungrateful" meaning, according to the codes of this culture, any slave who does not want to be a slave, and "nigger" being the crucial term on which the right of white people to own human beings rests. Like Tom's picturesque robbers, in other words, "nigger" is a created fiction rather than something you can see with your own eyes. When it comes to the culture's unwritten but pervasive conventions about race and slavery, however, Huck *does* see what is not there: he sees all too clearly, for example, how wrong he is to help Jim escape. The question of his freedom comes to depend on the possibility of shaking off this ideological illusion, on seeing Jim through his own eyes.

Twain himself refers to this thematic conflict in different terms in a journal entry from 1895 in which he calls *Huck Finn* "a book of mine where a sound heart & a deformed conscience come into collision & conscience suffers defeat."[9] By "deformed" Twain means formed by the corrupt social environment in which Huck has grown up. This is a realist's definition of conscience: its standards of right and wrong are not derived from any transhistorical, absolute moral realm, but rather acquired from culture. Whenever Huck's conscience torments him for helping Jim, it speaks with a southern accent, not a heavenly one; as Twain goes on to say in his journal, "the conscience . . . can be trained to approve any wild thing you *want* it to approve if you begin its education early & stick to it." In recording that this conscience suffers a defeat in *Huck Finn*, Twain must be thinking of the novel's best known scene, the passage in chapter 31 where Huck resolves to "*go* to hell" rather than turn Jim over to Miss Watson. As most commentary on the novel agrees, this scene forms its emotional and thematic climax, for it is most dramatically and insightfully here, with Jim imprisoned at the Phelpses' and Huck alone on the raft, that we take the full measure of both the power of society to enslave the mind and the possibility for an individual to resist that conditioning.

As Henry Nash Smith was the first to point out, the novel stages this collision as a kind of dialogue between two very different types of language.[10] The dialogue, like the dramatic conflict, occurs entirely within Huck's consciousness. There is the voice of his conscience, which speaks in the grandiloquent abstractions by means of which the self-interest of the ruling class is made to seem godlike and righteous:

> it hit me all of a sudden that here was the plain hand of Providence slapping me in the face and letting me know my wickedness was being watched all the time from up there in heaven, whilst I was stealing a poor old woman's nigger that hadn't ever done me no harm. (268–9)

Note how the rhetorical emphasis here falls on words that refer to things Huck has never seen: "hand of Providence," "up there in heaven." Opposed to this is the voice that Smith identifies as Huck's own vernacular one; the words this voice uses all come from the world that Huck himself has seen. It is this vernacular voice that, in one of the greatest ironies in literature, talks Huck into going to hell. We can hear both voices, and hear how the vernacular displaces the socially sanctioned one, in the long paragraph tracing Huck's thoughts after he has decided to "do the right thing" and write Miss Watson:

> I felt good and all washed clean of sin for the first time I had ever felt so in my life, and I knowed I could pray, now. But I didn't do it straight off, but laid the paper down and set there thinking; thinking how good it was all this happened so, and how near I come to being lost and going to hell. And went on thinking. And got to thinking over our trip down the river; and I see Jim before me, all the time, in the day, and in the night-time, sometimes moonlight, sometimes storms, and we a floating along, talking, and singing, and laughing. But somehow I

couldn't seem to strike no places to harden me against him, but only the other kind. (269–70)

This beautifully cadenced passage, which goes on for another one hundred fifty words, climaxes in Huck's decision to tear up the letter, and do the *wrong* thing: stand by his friend, "steal Jim out of slavery again" (271).

Twain's irony – that in a corrupt world moral salvation may depend on going to hell – is likely never to lose its dazzling potency. But the episode does leave a couple questions that should be asked, especially if we compare what happens in the novel with what Twain says happens in that journal entry he wrote ten years later. First, can we call Huck's choice a "defeat" of conscience? If it is, it is a very partial one. The unseen heaven and hell remain fixed in the places where the culture told Huck they are. He remains convinced that slavery is right and he is wrong, indeed that he is "wicked." Worst of all, he does not decide to "free" Jim but to "steal" him, which leaves intact the fundamental deformity of his slave-owning society: defining people as things that can be owned. Chapter 31 is as close as Huck will get to the state of mind that would free him. I think the most that can be said is that his experience fights his conscience to a tie.

The other question that must be asked is: should we accept Twain's explanation of the source of the voice and the values that resist the deformed conscience – Huck's "sound heart"? If so, Twain becomes more Romantic than Realist, for this idea of an innate, intuitive, uncontingent self is the source of the power on which writers like Jean Jacques Rousseau, William Wordsworth and Ralph Waldo Emerson base their programs of individual and societal redemption. *Huck Finn* appropriates a number of Romantic tropes, including the opposition between the realms of "nature" (the great river) and "society" (the dirty little villages on the shore), but its representation of life has more in common with our chastened 21st-century understanding of the dependency of selves on cultural discourse and environmental circumstances than with Romanticism's divine Self. The voice of Huck's "heart" is, like the voice of his "conscience," like all language, acquired from other people, learned, not intuitive. We know where his conscience learned its script – from the adult Christian slave-owning society of St Petersburg. Huck learned the vernacular in a lot of places, but he himself tells us specifically where the voice that disrupts the harangue of conscience in chapter 31 comes from: "our trip down the river." *Our* trip. It doesn't simply well up from the self, or from the river. It comes, as he also tells us, from his experience with his friend: "I see Jim before me."

This is why the novel is ultimately less about whether Huck can help free Jim than about whether Jim can help free Huck. On seeing Jim – seeing who *is* there, to echo that first line of dialogue – depends the possibility of Huck's emancipation from the ideological preconceptions he wears as his mental chains. The conflict in chapter 31 between what his own experience and his social conditioning tell him comes down very powerfully to a conflict between two particular words: "Jim" and "nigger." The passage begins with Huck thinking about "Jim," about what would be best for him as a person, "as long as he'd *got* to be a slave." Yet when he thinks of writing the note to Miss Watson that would return Jim back "home where his family was," he realizes what he would have to face himself: "It would get all around, that Huck Finn helped a nigger to get his freedom." Huck's sudden use of his own name instead of the "I" we have grown so accustomed to reveals that he is seeing himself through other people's eyes, re-viewing his experience according to St Petersburg's standards of judgment. Although alone on the raft, he remains bound to the ideological terms laid down by his society. Among the most crucial of those terms is the one that suddenly replaces "Jim" here, the word "nigger." In the novel's perfectly controlled depiction of Huck's thoughts during this crisis, Jim the man Huck knows disappears behind this cultural construct, becomes the thing society has told Huck is there: "a poor old woman's nigger," "that nigger." As the novel pounds that word into us here – Jim is referred to as an anonymous "nigger" five times in three paragraphs – we feel how much is lost when a human being is replaced by an abstraction, a racist label. But then when Huck stops thinking about St Petersburg's "sayings" and instead remembers his own experience on the raft on the river, a wonderful act of revision occurs: "I see Jim before me." In the long passage I quoted earlier, he remembers what he has seen for himself; the person Jim steps back in front of the label society has pinned to him.

Huck of course does not know he is enslaved. Nor does he get the meaning of his own story. In fact, its meaning can be said to reside in the way Huck doesn't understand the story he's telling: Huck's failure from beginning to end to see that the help he gives Jim is not a sin enables Twain ironically to dramatize the pervasive influence of ideology, what he will come to call "training." As the story of the quest for *Huck's* possible freedom, the novel thus connects the history of American slavery up with the psychology of racism. The habits of Huck's mind as conditioned by the social environment of the slave-owning village are deeply racist. "Niggers is always talking about witches" (8), "you can't learn a nigger to argue" (98) – he has been brought up to take these derogatory stereotypical prejudices as axiomatic truths. Twain even gives us scenes in which we can see for ourselves how white adults nurture this racism. There is Pap's drunken rant against free blacks, for example (33–4). More chillingly, there is this brief exchange between Huck and Aunt Sally, after she asks whether "anybody" was hurt in a steamboat explosion. "No'm," Huck replies, "Killed a nigger." "Well, that's lucky," Sally says, "because sometimes people do get hurt" (279). Neither Huck nor Sally even notice the way they deny that blacks are human beings, and dismiss the death of a slave as completely meaningless.

Pap's rant comes early in the novel; the conversation with Sally, from near the end. Readers must decide for themselves if over the course of the novel Huck is able to see through this pervasive racism. Between his stays with Pap and Sally comes the trip with Jim. Because the raft provides a space outside the slave-owning society where for much of the trip Huck is alone with Jim, the trip offers a chance, as Twain said of *his* travels in *Innocents Abroad*, "to unlearn a great many things [he has] somehow absorbed."[11] The Jim Huck gets to know on the raft does at times confound the stereotypes he has been taught. Hearing Jim crying for the family he had to leave behind, for example, Huck decides that "I do believe he cared just as much for his people as white folks does for theirn. It don't seem natural, but I reckon it's so" (201). This from Huck! whose experience of whites as parents has been Pap's vicious abuse. But in the way Huck uses "natural" we can hear again how powerful is the social construction of "reality" – the myth of white supremacy, like the existence of slavery, is for him simply "natural," part of the unchanging essence of things. There are a number of other moments with Jim when Huck seems on the verge of breaking through the deformed patterns of his training, but they don't necessarily add up to any demonstrable change. This is another interpretive issue that readers will always come to different conclusions about, whether Huck grows in the course of his "adventures." Generically, as the story of a youth leaving home to encounter the larger world, it certainly sets up the expectation that the arc of its narrative will be a learning curve. Structurally, on the other hand, as the ironic, deadpan first-person account by a narrator who doesn't appreciate the meaning of what he's telling us, it seems bound to maintain Huck's naivete. Without question, most of the hundreds of students to whom I've taught the book want to believe that by the end Huck has made real progress toward freedom from the most vicious aspects of society. To them, and to many of the novel's scholarly analysts, Huck's announcement on the last page that he is going "to light out for the Territory" rather than allow Aunt Sally to adopt him amounts to a principled rejection of "sivilization" (362). On the other hand, on the novel's first page Huck tells us that he has already "lit out" from the Widow's attempt to adopt him (1). Throughout we see the same kinds of repetition, without any clear sign of progress: for example, Huck's confrontation with his conscience in chapter 31 is essentially the same as the one he has in chapter 16. Throughout the novel is testing the idea of escaping one's acculturation: the raft on the river is much the same kind of setting as the Territory. Since Huck carries the standards and prejudices of his society inside his consciousness, it's not clear how physical escape could bring him any closer to a perception of reality "un-deformed" by the "old sayings" he has been brought up on.

Read as Huck's triumph over society, his lighting out into the west becomes Twain's reaffirmation of the Romantic faith in the possibility of going to nature as a means of beginning anew, outside the fallen realms of society and history. We could even read it as his reinvigoration of the myth on which America's idea of itself is still deeply based: that by going west, into a new world, humanity can break the chains that have historically imprisoned them. Part of the power *Huck Finn* has as a classic American novel comes, without doubt, from the way it invites us to read it as a valorization of the promise of individual freedom. If, however, we come to the conclusion, however reluctantly, that Huck does not seem any freer on the last page than he was on the first, the novel nevertheless does suggest how freedom could be attained. It does not depend on anything so mystical as a "sound heart," but rather on keeping oneself open to one's own experience, on seeing what, and who, is really there. Thus

Twain's project as a Realist can, in its own way, provide the basis for a new, re-formed, more democratic community. For as we can see in chapter 31, although there Huck is by himself on the raft, finally his freedom is not expressed in the image of an individual alone in nature, but rather, as "I see Jim before me" beautifully puts it, in the relationship between two human beings – one white, one black – seeking freedom together.

The novel's emphasis on racism is why it was still entirely pertinent when Twain wrote it in the second decade after slavery had been abolished, and why it remains relevant today, as America continues to struggle out of the shadow cast by slavery and the racist ideology that slavery made necessary. But is *Huck Finn* part of the solution or part of the problem? For the past quarter century that has been the subject of a heated debate. To the people who are actively campaigning to ban it from classrooms, the novel is, as John Wallace has repeatedly charged, "the most grotesque example of racist trash ever written."[12] To its defenders, it is, as Mesach Taylor said on ABC TV's *Nightline* in 1985, "one of the best indictments against racism in the United States."[13] As this controversy has played out in the media, it has focused on Huck's use, 212 times, of the word "nigger" to describe African Americans. One valuable result of the protest has been, I hope, to make all of us who teach the novel more sensitive to the real anguish that word can cause students who are being required to read it. But while Huck uses the term unthinkingly, the novel knows and wants us to think about what his use of it means. One of Twain's great themes is the role language plays in creating "reality." When Huck is at the Wilkses, Joanna asks him to swear he's telling the truth on a big book that turns out to be a dictionary rather than the Bible (cf. 224); that is one of the ways the novel asks us to pay careful attention to words and definitions. Whenever Tom Sawyer is with Huck, the theme is rendered comically, as Tom tries to impose the terms he finds in European romances on American circumstances: a "pick-axe," for instance, has to be called a "case-knife" before it can be used to help a prisoner escape (307) and the right name for "mullen" in those circumstances is "Pitchiola" (327). But the more time Huck spends with Jim, the more palpably the reader can see that the names one uses to articulate the world can have potentially tragic consequences. "Nigger" is what you have to call a human being to legitimize enslaving him, but in its best moments, as in that passage from chapter 31, the novel reveals how terribly the term "nigger" misdefines Jim.

Yet *Huck Finn*'s contemporary critics have good cause to accuse the novel of racism. The problem is not what Huck calls Jim, but how the novel itself represents Jim. The way Huck "sees Jim" in chapter 31 is not the narrative's only or even its last representation of him: the human face he wears there is in other scenes replaced by the blackface image of the minstrel show clown. It's as if there are two "Jim's" in the story. In the middle chapters he often appears as intelligent, re-sourceful, enterprising, caring, even proud and dignified, as in the wonderful scene in chapter 15 where he rebukes Huck for "mak[ing] a fool uv ole Jim wid a lie" (105), a scene in which Jim also, with great moral clarity, redefines what makes people "trash." But at the beginning of the story, and especially at the end, in the long episode at the Phelpses' in which Tom takes over the plot, the role Jim plays is entirely stereotypical. It is a very bleak irony that when the narra-tive finally focuses on the quest that has served since chapter 8 to keep it in motion – the quest to free Jim – it does so in a way that does more than trivialize the quest; the more the boys play at freeing Jim, the more it is the narrative itself that effectively re-enslaves him, by re-inscribing on his character the racist image of the "happy darky." The bleakest part of the irony is that this happens after (in the novel) Miss Watson has already freed Jim, and after (in the America Twain is writing for) all slaves have been legally emancipated. When *Huck Finn* was published, slavery no longer stood between blacks and freedom, but racial segregation and racist stereotyping did. White America (with the help, of course, of several hundred thousand black Union sol-diers) abolished slavery, but then refused to take seriously the rights of African Americans to equal participation in society.

The concluding episode of *Huck Finn* has troubled readers since the 1920s. In his tribute to the novel, Hemingway warns that "you must stop" before reading those chapters. A growing number of critics now suggest that the Phelps' episode should be read as an angry satire in which Twain is critiquing the failure of Reconstruction and the subse-quent disenfranchisement of blacks under Jim Crow.[14] Twain expects his readers, in other words, to see the way Tom abuses Jim not just as wrong, but as a quasi-allegorical equivalent to what the majority white culture was aggressively doing to the freed black men and women in the South at the time the novel was published. There is no doubt that such an interpretation serves the needs of critics in our time, anxious to recuperate this classic American novel from the stigma of racism. There is, however, not the faintest hint of contextual evidence that any reader in Twain's time took the ending this way, while there is a lot of evidence to suggest that Twain himself expected and encouraged his audience to enjoy the ending as slapstick, not satire – which, we can prove, is what they did.

As the publication date of *Huck Finn* neared, Twain wrote the man in charge of publishing it to say "There is not going to be any reason whatever, why this book shall not succeed – & it shall & it *must*."[15] To help promote it Twain arranged to go back on the lecture tour for the first time in a dozen years, and included excerpts from the forthcoming novel in his performance. During the first half of the tour he featured Huck and Jim's minstrel-like conversations about "speculatin' in stock" and "King Sollermun" (chapters 8 and 14), but when the tour took a week-long Christmas break he revamped his routine to make "the episode where Tom & Huck stock Jim's cabin with reptiles, & then set him free"[16] its main feature. Thus Mark Twain actually performed the ending of *Huck Finn* live about fifty times before over 10,000 members of his contemporary public. In the letters he wrote Livy after each performance we can hear both the audiences' enjoyment of the episode and Twain's pride in his ability to entertain them: "it's the biggest card I've got in my whole repetoire," he reported from Pittsburgh, and from Chicago he boasted that "Tom & Huck setting Jim free from prison . . . just went with a long roll of artillery-laughter all down the line, . . . from the first word to the last."[17] Newspaper reviews of the tour confirm these accounts: "In his next selection he read a chapter of his unpublished book 'Huckleberry Finn,'" noted the Cincinnati *Enquirer*, "explaining how 'Huck' and 'Tom Sawyer' freed the runaway 'nigger,' which created roars of laughter"; the audience, said the Indianapolis *Journal*, was "tickled to death with the story of Huck Finn and Tom Sawyer in their arrangement of 'Jim's' escape from the cabin."[18]

Huck Finn was the first book brought out by the subscription publishing company that Twain founded in 1884. As the owner of the company, he had complete creative control over the way the novel was designed and marketed. He was, as Walter Blair puts it, "indefatigable in directing every step" of the book's production,[19] and all the choices he made show the same ambition we hear in his comments on enacting the novel before live audiences: the goal of entertaining readers, even at the expense of denying the revisionary ambition behind *Huck Finn*. It was promoted, for example, as a "companion" to *The Adventures of Tom Sawyer*: it deliberately used the same layout, and its subtitle, "Tom Sawyer's Comrade," was displayed prominently in all the advertisements. Similarly the ad campaign promised Americans a book "in the same vein" and in "Mark Twain's old style of writing." Like the self-deprecatory "Notice" Twain wrote to precede the text, ads assured readers that there was nothing in the novel to trouble or challenge them. It was "a mine of humor," pure and simple.[20]

The book's original illustrations tell the same story of an author anxious to ingratiate himself with his audience. Twain himself picked E. W. Kemble to draw the copious illustrations that subscription buyers expected. After reviewing the first batch Kemble sent, however, he expressed uneasiness that Kemble's representations of the characters were not "pleasant folk to look at" and advised that an "artist shouldn't follow a book too literally, perhaps."[21] In other words, he would rather have the illustrations misrepresent the text than risk alienating readers. There was only one illustration he vetoed: Kemble's drawing of the King kissing a pretty girl at the camp meeting in chapter 20. Twain liked the picture a lot, but again indicated that he was counting on the illustrations to disguise the "truth" of the novel: "It is powerful good, but it mustn't go in . . . Let's not make *any* pictures of the campmeeting . . . pictures are sure to tell the truth about it too plainly."[22] With this kind of thinking Twain is obviously in full retreat from everything that realism is supposed to stand for, and what he himself has written. He is asking Kemble to take the story Huck tells (which is full of things that are "awful to see") and turn it into one that will be "pleasant to look at."

Twain seems not to have made any objections to Kemble's representation of Jim or the other African American characters, although to us the images look blatantly racist. Whenever Jim appears his mouth hangs open beneath eyes that are impossibly big and white: this is the mask of the minstrel show "darky" (see Figure 4). Even at a moment like the scene where Jim offers to risk his recovered liberty for the sake of Tom's safety, Kemble's illustration depicts him as the same unchanging clown (see Figure 5). To the casual reader, whose responses are being guided by the pictures that occupy so much space

"BY RIGHTS I AM A DUKE!"

FIGURE 4   Illustration by E. W. Kemble for page 163, *Adventures of Huckleberry Finn* (New York: Charles L. Webster and Company, 1885)

JIM ADVISES A DOCTOR.

FIGURE 5   Illustration by E. W. Kemble for page 345, *Adventures of Huckleberry Finn* (New York: Charles L. Webster and Company, 1885)

on the pages of the book, the grotesquely comic role that the narrative writes for Jim to play at the Phelpses' is no different from the way he appears throughout the story. The novel's acute analysis of the difference between real people and cultural stereotypes goes entirely unrecorded in the illustrations, which refuse to give Jim any hint of emotional or intellectual complexity. As he is drawn, Jim never has a chance to be seen as a human being.

Beginning with his work on *Huck Finn*, and then for the next forty years, "Kemble's coons," as his representations of African Americans were called, were very popular with the white reading public[23] – and for reasons that are not difficult to apprehend. His blackface caricatures make no moral demands on the majority culture; laughing at them exorcises any anxiety or guilt whites might feel about the inferior place freed men and women were forced to occupy in a segregated nation. It's likely that when contempoary readers got to the ending Twain wrote for *Huck Finn*, far from seeing or even sensing it as a critique of America's deformed racial politics, they felt similarly let off the hook. The situation Twain sets up when Tom reappears – which Huck refers to, crudely, as "set[ting] a free nigger free" (358) – is the issue that America faced at the time he wrote the novel. By treating it as the occasion for a farce, by turning Jim at the end into the "darky" Kemble's drawings show readers from the beginning, Twain allows his audience to laugh away the rights and wrongs of blacks. Jim is in fact portrayed as "happy" about the novel's last episode; when the escapees reach the raft, and Huck tells him that he's "a free man *again*," Jim endorses what Tom has done to him: "En a mighty good job it wuz, too, Huck. It 'uz planned beautiful, en it 'uz *done* beautiful" (340). One scene Twain doesn't include is when Jim later finds out that he was a free man all the time Tom was using him as a prop in his romantic shenanigans. Given his eloquent reponse to the way Huck tried to make a fool of him after the fog in chapter 15, Jim might have had something equally heroic to say about the "lie" that underlies Tom's actions, about the injustice of denying him his true freedom, something Twain's American audience badly needed to hear. Instead of that scene, however, the narrative gives us his "happy darky" response to the forty dollars Tom gives him as reparation for "being prisoner for us": "I tole you . . . [I] gwineter be rich *agin*; en it's come true" (361).

For once, Tom Sawyer seems to get a label right when he tells Huck that what they're doing to Jim is "called an evasion" (333). We could call what Twain is doing an *un*-writing. He began *Huck Finn* with the ambition to un-write *Tom Sawyer*, but with the end of the novel he un-writes *Huck Finn as Tom Sawyer*. Not only does Tom come back into the narrative, bringing with him the aesthetic of play rather than the life-and-death realities Huck has confronted during his journey with Jim; at the same time Huck becomes "Tom Sawyer." That is his name at the Phelpses'. At the end of chapter 31 he bravely decides to go to hell for his friend, but when he gets to the plantation where Jim is being held for a reward Huck finds that the Phelpses are expecting Tom Sawyer. So he (and Twain) give them (and Twain's readers) Tom Sawyer. "Being Tom Sawyer was easy and comfortable," Huck notes; "it was like being born again" to have that role to play (282). The ending of *Huck Finn* disturbs modern readers, because in our minds Twain is a major author and Jim a human being. The same ending delighted Twain's contemporaries, because they thought of Twain as an entertainer and saw Jim through their preconceptions about blacks as characters: from both "Mark Twain" and black characters, they expected something to laugh at, and that is what the Phelps episode works so hard to give them. Snakes, rats, spiders, mashed teeth, an absent-minded uncle, an easily-flustered aunt – the narrative keeps the physical comedy constantly in motion. By making his readers laugh, Twain allows them to evade the serious questions about race, history and society raised by the novel's earlier chapters. By satisfying their expectations, however, he effectively sells out his own story. So in the end, Huck cannot free Jim from slavery (Miss Watson does that, offstage), nor can Jim free Huck from his deformed conscience – and neither can *Huck Finn* free "Mark Twain" from his image as a humorist, from his need for popular approval.

Twain's heightened sensitivity to the bonds by which he was tied to his audience may explain the presence of the King and the Duke in the novel's second half. These two con men are always putting on some kind of performance for an audience, from conventional shows for which they rent a theater and sell tickets to their masquerades as a pirate at a camp meeting or as the Wilks brothers. Huck, as we noted in the last chapter, hates attention himself, and so gives the narrative a way to stand outside the performance and watch both the actors and the audiences. What he sees revises the rosy account of performing that was so central in *Tom Sawyer*. In *Tom Sawyer* the shows Tom puts on to satisfy his obsessive need for attention can be legitimately heroic too. In *Huck Finn*, however, performing is represented as a series of cons in which the entertainers exploit the worst appetites of the people in the audience for the most sordid of motives. The people of Bricksville, for example, are uninterested in Shakespeare. "What they wanted was low comedy – and maybe something worse" (194). Huck describes them as they flock to the Royal Nonesuch, and as they "squirm and scrounge and push and shove" for a front-row view of a dying man (187) or laugh "till the tears rolled down" at what they think is a drunken man being tossed around by a dangerous horse (193). In *Huck Finn* the art of popular performance is another thing that becomes "awful to see," and its masters are the despicable King and Duke. Whether the King is playing the role of reformed pirate, telling the "dear people" of Pokeville that they are "natural brothers and benefactors of the race" (173), or the part of Harvey Wilks telling the people of another village that his supposed brother's funeral will be public because "he respected everybody, he liked everybody" (217), the one line he never forgets is telling his audience how great they are. The secret of the King and Duke's ability to manipulate audiences lies in the fact that they never tell them the truth but rather feed their appetites and flatter their prejudices.

The antithesis of the kind of show they put on is the lecture Colonel Sherburn delivers to the Bricksville mob that wants to lynch him. Standing above the crowd on the roof of his house, holding a rifle and laughing contemptuously at his audience, he stages an anti-entertainment: in his "slow and scornful" voice he tells them the truth about themselves, "what you are" (190), attacking rather than flattering their self-complacency. Although Huck is nothing like Sherburn, in some ways Twain began the novel with the design of using Huck's voice to tell a similar kind of truth about American society, especially the idealized image of the slave-holding past he had helped perpetuate in *Tom Sawyer*. Being Huck Finn was by no means "easy and comfortable," but writing a novel from within that character was a way to push at the limits of his role as a popular writer, and to challenge the readers he had grown tired of merely entertaining. But Sherburn is hated for the truth he tells, and Twain finally was not willing to risk the love of his audience for the chance at imaginative freedom. That he chose to re-ingratiate himself with white Americans by playing the race card, that he decided to write the Evasion section and make his readers happy by making Jim and *his* quest for freedom ridiculous, tells us a truth about our cultural history that makes us uncomfortable. Hence the zealousness of the critics who refuse to see anything racist about *Huck Finn*. Yet what the novel can tell us about our past and our selves is vital for us to know, which is why the campaign to ban the book from classrooms, while understandable, is misguided. It should be taught, but as a text that embodies both the best and the worst of our culture. The Phelps section is "something ruther worse than low comedy": it is one of American literature's most dramatic and painful examples of how we have denied the meaning of our own history as well as the rightful place of former slaves. But the novel also gives us the fragile but real inspiration of the image of the raft on the river, carrying two fugitives toward a freedom that has yet to be attained and the hope of a truly just and democratic community.

That possibility is not completely destroyed when the King and Duke come on board the raft, nor wholly erased when Twain writes the Evasion episode and himself puts on a show that the King and Duke would have admired. Yet the way the novel identifies performance and popularity with the fraudulent manipulations of two sordid con men does suggest that, as much as he wanted the book to be popular, Twain would have deep misgivings about his own success. That in turn might explain his surprising desire at the time *Huck Finn* came out to retire as a publishing author. The decade between 1876, when he began writing *Huck Finn* and *Tom Sawyer* was published, and 1885, when *Huck Finn* at last went on sale, was in many respects the most productive of Twain's career. During those years, in addition to many short pieces, he published another novel, *The Prince and the Pauper* (1881), and two long travel books, *A Tramp Abroad* (1880) and *Life on the Mississippi* (1883). Life in his Hartford home with Livy and, by 1880, his three daughters was emotionally full and satisfying for most of this period too. *Huck Finn* took longer to finish than any of his other works: he wrote about a quarter of it in that first burst of inspiration, summer of 1876, came back to the manuscript to write the two Grangerford chapters in 1880, then in 1883 took it up and finished it. Huck is certainly speaking for his creator when, on the last page, he talks about "what a trouble it was to make a book" (362). Huck was also speaking for some part of Twain when he adds that he "ain't agoing to no more" – that he won't tackle writing any more books. At least, Twain began telling acquaintances not long after *Huck*

Finn appeared, to mixed reviews but great sales figures, that it was the last book he would ever publish. They never took this assertion too seriously, and in fact he continued to write. But he also had begun to look for other ways to make money from the written word. While the first book released by his own publishing company was *Huck Finn*, he soon was adding many other authors to firm's list. More ominously, he was investing more and more of the money he made from his imagination in the invention of a man named James Paige: the invention was a typesetting machine that Twain believed would make him fabulously rich. Publishing *company*, typesetting *machine* – if these ventures paid off, he would no longer have to write or un-write any books himself. In that case, if he did feel he had betrayed Huck, Jim and himself by turning *Huck Finn* into *Tom Sawyer*, he would no longer have to perform at all for his reading public. The ventures did not pay off, and Twain wrote and published many more books. But public performance, as we will see, is often what these later works are preoccupied with.

Lost in Time
A Connecticut Yankee in King Arthur's Court

In *Innocents Abroad*, his first book about going east to the old world, Mark Twain describes a revelation he had in the Holy Land. Presbyterian pilgrims, he observed, "found a Presbyterian Palestine," Baptists "seeking Baptist evidences . . . found a Baptist Palestine," and there was also "a Catholic, a Methodist, an Episcopalian Palestine," depending on each sightseer's prejudices and perspective.[1] This is the kind of revelation that makes someone a skeptic rather than a believer, but while the complex nature of the relationship between perception and interpretation, between seeing and understanding the world, is an issue he explores throughout his works, he began his career with the belief that there was such a thing as reality itself, which he could use as both a humorist and a serious writer to burlesque or expose delusions and shams. *Adventures of Huckleberry Finn* is his most brilliant testimony to that belief, which burns brightest in the scenes where Huck can, as he puts it, "see Jim before me" *as he is*, apart from the racial prejudices Huck's cultural conditioning has put between him and all black people. In the works Twain wrote after *Huck Finn*, however, "reality" becomes an increasingly problematic concept. The erosion of this bedrock on which the project of literary realism is built culminates in the ending that Twain wrote for one version of the "Mysterious Stranger," the story that haunted him during the last decade of his life: "*Life itself is only a vision, a dream*," the supernatural character called No. 44 tells the narrator; "*Nothing* exists; all is a dream."[2]

The Mysterious Stranger, like most of Twain's late fiction, was published posthumously, so his contemporaries never read his philosophically most pessimistic works. If they had been reading more carefully, however, they could have found much in the books and short pieces he did publish to disturb their image of "Mark Twain" as genial and beloved humorist. As the nation's first literary celebrity, that image grew steadily more and more familiar to America, indeed to the world. Inside that image, however, reality and his own success became increasingly strange to the man who wore "Mark Twain" as his public identity. These ambivalences come to occupy the center of much that "Mark Twain" wrote. His next book after *Huck Finn* was *A Connecticut Yankee in King Arthur's Court*, another account of going east to an old world. Like those pilgrims to Palestine, different readers have read this novel very differently. To his nineteenth-century contemporaries, the novel was Twain's patriotic critique of the European past, and Hank Morgan, the Yankee, was an entirely reliable as well as sympathetic first-person narrator. Modern readers, however, are more likely to read it as an unreliable or ironic first-person narrative that ultimately expresses Twain's deep misgivings about the American present. In various ways it is both those books. To me, it is also an autobiographical parable about Twain's conflicted ambitions and frustrations as an American celebrity, a performing writer; in a way I'll try to explain, it is Twain's disguised commentary on his own career.

Published in 1889, *Connecticut Yankee* developed from an idea Twain entered into his journal in December, 1884. While in the middle of the lecture tour he arranged to promote *Huck Finn*'s publication, his imagination was caught by the idea of being trapped inside a shell:

> Dream of being a knight errant in armor in the middle ages.
>
> Have the notions & habits of thought of the present day mixed with the necessities of that. No pockets in the armor. No way to manage certain requirements of nature. Can't scratch . . . can't blow [nose] . . . Suffer from lice & fleas . . . See Morte Darthur.[3]

We should note the prominence of the concept of "dreaming" here, although in this context it doesn't seem at all ominous. Instead, this idea strikes us as a particulary inspired example of the sort of comic situation Twain loved. As a humorist, he confessed in one of his autobiographical dictations, "I have always preached"[4]; laughter, Satan tells the narrator of another of the "Mysterious Stranger" manuscripts, is mankind's best weapon against "humbugs" of all kinds: "Against the assault of Laughter nothing can stand."[5] His uncomfortable knight is burlesque with a purpose, physical comedy with its roots in democratic principles (making a titled knight laughable subverts the idea of class superiority) and in realistic aesthetics (giving this knight an itchy body and a runny nose demystifies the idealizations of romance). As he had done with the "Old Masters" in *Innocents Abroad*, for example, he is using humor to topple the idols his society worshipped. Contemporary guardians of traditional values often accused Twain of irreverent vulgarity when he engaged in this kind of debunking, as when in the 1877 "Whittier Birthday Dinner Speech" he took three champions of American High Culture – Ralph Waldo Emerson, Oliver Wendell Holmes and Henry Wadsworth Longfellow – and transformed them into three unwashed tramps. But as humorists have always known, making the sacred look silly is a dependable way to make audiences uncomfortable enough to laugh, and a major component of Twain's popularity with the mass American audience was the way he targeted elite or aristocratic subjects.

As "See Morte Darthur" suggests, behind this idea for a humorous text are other texts. *Le Morte d'Arthur*, a collection of tales about the chivalrous adventures of the knights of the Round Table, was written in the 15th century by Sir Thomas Malory. Not long before making that journal entry Twain had been given a copy of the book by George Washington Cable, with whom he shared the stage on the *Huck Finn* promotional tour. *Connecticut Yankee* engages directly in the act of un-writing Malory's book: long passages of Malory's stately, archaic prose appear alongside Hank Morgan's colloquially American narration. But Twain's deeper quarrel is with the 19th century writers who perpetuate the vision and the values of Malory's romance in the present day. Alfred Lord Tennyson's *Idylls of the King* (1859–85), for example, translated Malory's prose romance into best-selling Victorian poetry. And "Great Scott" is not only Hank's favorite expletive, but also Twain's way of reminding his readers of Sir Walter Scott, whose historical romances about knights and ladies, like *Ivanhoe* (1819), remained very popular with readers on both sides of the Atlantic at the time Twain decided to un-write the legend of Camelot. Although Scott died before Sam Clemens was born, and although as a young reader Clemens loved Scott's books, as a writer Twain hated Scott – partly as a rival for the attention of the reading public, but also on principle as a benighted writer of romance. Speaking in his own voice as "Mark Twain" in *Life on the Mississippi*, he accuses Scott of doing "measureless harm; more real and lasting harm, perhaps, than any other individual that ever wrote." The French Revolution at the end of the 18th century, Twain explains, made a great leap forward for the interests of "liberty, humanity, and progress" –

> Then comes Sir Walter Scott with his enchantments, and by his single might checks this wave of progress, and even turns it back; sets the world in love with dreams and phantoms; with decayed and swinish forms of religion; with decayed and degraded systems of government; with the sillinesses and emptinesses, sham grandeurs, sham gauds, and sham chivalries of a brainless and worthless long-vanished society.[6]

The assumption here is one Twain shared with other realist writers like Gustave Flaubert, who made Emma Bovary an avid reader of romances, and even had her attend an opera based on one of Scott's books: that is, that reading can be dangerous, that unrealistic fictions can distort people's expectations about reality. In Twain's case, this concern was given particular force by the social circumstances that, as Sam Clemens growing up in Missouri, he knew firsthand: the role that Scott's medieval romances played in the American South. The "Sir Walter disease," he claims, was "in great measure responsible for the [Civil W]ar," and even now, in the 1880s, in the South "the genuine and wholesome civilization of the nineteenth-century is curiously confused and commingled with the Walter Scott Middle-Age sham civilization."

In these remarks we can hear not only how good a hater Twain was, but also the patterns that connect Hank up with Huck, whose freedom depends on throwing off the ideological fictions of southern society. Like Huck, Hank gives Twain a realistic narrative vantage point outside the culture he moves through, a habit of looking that will not succumb to the enchantments and idealizations on which literary romance thrives, a way, in other words, of seeing what is "really there." Hank points toward the kind of book that Twain is using him to write in a passage that, though it doesn't mention Scott by name, recalls what *Life on the Mississippi* says about the French Revolution and then adds that the "real" Reign of Terror is the long history of European feudalism that the Revolution rose up to destroy: "that older and real Terror – that unspeakably bitter and awful Terror which none of us has been taught to see in its vastness or pity as it deserves."[7] Despite its fantastic premise – it is probably the world's first novel about time-travel[8] – *Connecticut Yankee* has a realist agenda. As he himself had done in *Innocents Abroad*, Twain sends Hank to the Old World to teach readers the truths that other books leave out, to show them the facts that other books falsify.

Hank's credentials for this job are similar to Huck's. Hank is not illiterate, but in his introductory description of himself as "a Yankee of the Yankees" he too defines himself in opposition to popular literary culture, as "nearly barren of sentiment, I suppose – or poetry" (4). The antithesis to "poetic," in this passage, is "practical," which recalls Huck's habit, when the other characters tell him about the "truths" they know from books, of testing their assertions by his own experience: just as Huck rubs a lamp to see if one of Tom's genies will appear, so when the sacred fountain in the Valley of Holiness goes dry, Hank rejects the explanation that it has been enchanted by an evil spirit and instead lights a candle and goes into the well to "find out what was really the matter" for himself (210). His matter-of-fact way of seeing makes Hank a better guide than the romance writers to the social realities of King Arthur's England. When he is taken to Camelot for the first time, he sees "a noble cavalcade" of knights, "glorious with plumed helmets, and flashing mail, and flaunting banners" – but is not blinded by this aristocratic splendor to the squalor in which most of the population lives: he describes "the wretched cabins," "the muck, and swine," the impoverished and imbruted men, women and children over those lives the knights ride (11).

Through Hank's unsentimental eyes Twain's readers see the nobility as beautiful to look at, but also "tyrannical, murderous, rapacious, and morally rotten" (148). Twice in the narrative he takes long trips through the kingdom, and the sights he sees add up to a deliberate alternative to Malory's or Scott's or Tennyson's emphasis on deeds of chivalry. He descends into the dungeons beneath Morgan le Fay's picturesque castle to take inventory of what he calls the "legitimatest possible children of Monarchy by the Grace of God and the Established Church" (170), the imprisoned and tortured victims of the aristocratic system. He and Arthur are even sold into slavery, where they learn viscerally about the human misery that, for the novel, constitutes the real darkness of the Dark Ages. Hank's journeys through the sufferings, squalors and injustices of ordinary life in Arthurian

England resemble in some respects Huck's travels through the villages along the river, but unlike Huck, Hank is very consciously a critic of the society he encounters. "The most of King Arthur's British nation were slaves, pure and simple," he informs us, and then goes on, as a political analyst, to add that in the real world of the 6th century, most of "the rest were slaves in fact, but without the name" (65). Darkness is one of the novel's central tropes for feudal Europe; slavery is another. "A privileged class, an aristocracy," Hank asserts at one point, "is but a band of slave-holders under another name" (239). "Any Established Church," he proclaims at another, "is an established crime, an established slave-pen" (139–40).

We are a long way here from the idea for a humorous sketch Twain began with. *Connecticut Yankee* does contain slapstick, burlesque and other kinds of comedy; there is, for instance, a lengthy scene of Hank's miseries, the first time he is required to wear armor, from sweat, itches, insects and other anti-romantic nuisances (see 100–1, 107–8). But much of the novel is preaching without the humor, as Twain often allows Hank's voice to become righteous in its indignation against social evils. There are even a number of moments at which his sympathy for the plight of the common men and women gives way to a bitter contempt for them. Noting the privileges enjoyed by the aristocratic minority, six people "in each thousand of [the] population," Hank says that "what the nine hundred and ninety-four dupes needed was a new deal" (114). This is the passage that gave Franklin Roosevelt a name for his agenda during the Great Depression of the 1930s, but Hank not only says "new deal" – he also refers to common people as "dupes," and that is mild in comparison to many of his other epithets for them: "innumerable clams" (110), "human sheep" (114), even "human muck" (427).

Yet Twain can allow Hank to be angry and accusatory without much risk of alienating his readers. Although scorn for common people was not a note they associated with "Mark Twain," in this case it could be just as entertaining as his humor. The social evils and unthinking minds Hank condemns so aggressively belong to 6th century Europe; tearing them down is also a way of flattering the prejudices of his American contemporaries. Hank repeatedly reminds his readers that his critical point of view is that of a displaced but loyal "Yankee of the Yankees," "a person born in a wholesome free atmosphere" (63). Thus the enslavement of humanity in the European past is contrasted with the freedom enjoyed in the American present, just as the injustices of an aristocratic system are measured against a democratic one where are all equal before the law and power derives from the just consent of the governed, the evil of an established Catholic Church against Hank's experience with Protestantism and religious liberty in the United States, the ignorance of the 6th century population against the blessings of public education, the primitive superstitions of people who believe in magic against the technological achievements of a nation founded on science, reason, common-sense and a patent system that rewards initiative and invention. By sending Hank back east to condemn the old world past Americans came from, Twain is also vindicating the myth of the westward and progressive movement of the human race that puts the United States in the privileged place of being the world's last, best hope.

At least, this is certainly the way his publishing company promoted and advertised the book. The most prominent phrase on the poster Webster & Company designed to help subscription agents sell *Connecticut Yankee* calls it "A BOOK THAT APPEALS TO ALL TRUE AMERICANS."[9] The "Publisher's Announcement" develops this theme in terms that help us appreciate the cultural psychology of the appeal: "The book answers the Godly slurs that have been cast at us for generations by the titled gentry of England," prospective buyers are informed in the second paragraph, and at the end of the Announcement told that "the Yankee is constantly answering modern English criticism of America, and pointing out the weakness and injustice of government by a privileged class often mentally and physically far inferior to the masses of people over whom they rule." As we noted in chapter 1, Twain wrote before "the American century" established the nation as a world power in physical terms. Psychically, the nation still wrestled with a sense of cultural inferiority that is inevitably part of the heritage of a colonial society. For many, what the "Old Masters" Twain ridicules in *Innocents Abroad* were to art, "Camelot" was to human history: the chivalry, the courtesy, the nobility of its knights and ladies made it a superior moment from which present society had degenerated, and compared to which the raw democracy of Twain's America could seem a dystopian antithesis. Hank rides into the cultural lists as the champion of the modern, the democratic and the American. This happens literally in chapter 39, when riding a horse with a western saddle and swinging a lariat like a cowboy Hank defeats the best of that aristocratic world on their own ground (see Figure 6).

Hank's triumphant sense of national superiority is echoed by nearly all the novel's American reviewers. The novel, according to William Dean Howell's review in *Harper's Magazine*, "makes us glad of our republic and our epoch," and this self-gratulatory response is still more prominent in other American opinions. Sylvester Baxter, writing in the Boston *Herald* under the headline "Mark Twain's Masterwork," writes: "Throughout the book there is a steady flowing undercurrent of earnest purpose, and the pages are eloquent with a true American love of freedom, a sympathy with the rights of the common people, and an indignant hatred of oppression of the poor, the lowly and the weak, by the rich, the powerful and the proud." Out in California, in an anonyous review in the *Plumas National*, the flag-waving was even more overt:

> Mark Twain has come up from the people. He is American to the backbone, and the assumption of natural superiority by titled English aristocrats and the terrible wrongs inflicted on the working people, evidently galled him beyond endurance. He has taken his revenge in this volume . . . he has mercilessly flayed the follies, vices, cruelties and false pretensions of English royalty and aristocracy.

The novel did get one negative American review, from the Boston *Literary World*, whose unnamed critic agreed that the "serious aim under Mark Twain's travesty is the glorification of American Protestant democracy," but rejected the attempt for two reasons. First, like the British reviewers who almost without exception panned the novel, this critic condemned Twain's "flippancy and unmanly irreverence" toward the "grand heroisms of human history"; he was not prepared to encourage "one of the worst tendencies in a democratic State" by laughing at Lancelot, Galahad and company. Second, he thought the novel too smugly pro-American: "the effort fails through [its] extreme partiality."[10]

It is worth quoting the contemporary reviews, because from teaching *Connecticut Yankee* I have learned that modern readers have difficulty seeing the novel as its original audience did. Regardless of whether they like the book, those reviewers assume Twain intends Hank to be an admirable hero who speaks for Twain himself. Hank's smug

and grasped in his strong hand, his grand horse's face and breast
cased in steel, his body clothed in rich trappings that almost dragged
the ground—oh, a most noble picture. A great shout went up, of
welcome and admiration.

And then out I came. But I didn't get any shout. There was a
wondering and eloquent silence, for a moment, then a great wave of
laughter began to sweep along that human sea, but a warning bugle-
blast cut its career short. I was in the simplest
and comfortablest of gymnast costumes — flesh-
colored tights from neck to heel, with
blue silk puffings about my

loins, and bare-
headed. My horse
was not above
medium size, but
he was alert, slen-
der-limbed, muscled

"GO IT, SLIM JIM!"

with watch-springs, and just a greyhound to go. He was a beauty,
glossy as silk, and naked as he was when he was born, except for
bridle and ranger-saddle.

The iron tower and the gorgeous bed-quilt came cumbrously
but gracefully pirouetting down the lists, and we tripped lightly
up to meet them. We halted; the tower saluted, I responded;
then we wheeled and rode side by side to the grand stand and

FIGURE 6   Illustration by Dan Beard for page 499, *A Connecticut Yankee in
King Arthur's Court* (New York: Charles L. Webster and Company, 1889)

preference for "the genuine and wholesome civilization of the nineteenth century" over "a brainless and worthless . . . absurd past that is dead, and out of charity ought to be buried" certainly echoes what Twain says in *Life on the Mississippi*, from which these phrases are quoted. And Twain sounds like Hank in the notes on *Connecticut Yankee* he wrote for *The Century Magazine*, which published excerpts from the novel in November, 1889, as part of Twain's promotional campaign: the Yankee, he tells the magazine's readers, "has privately set himself the task of introducing the great and beneficent civilization of the nineteenth century, and of peacefully replacing the twin despotisms of royalty and aristocratic privilege with a 'Republic on the American plan.'"[11] But for good reasons, my students usually have serious reservations about Hank, and assume Twain is writing ironically, as he so often does with first-person narrators, from "Mark Twain" in "The Jumping Frog" to Huck Finn. For instance, Hank's determination to reshape a different culture according to his "American plan" looks less to them like salvation, bringing the light of Progress to the Dark Ages, than like the imperialist domination of a more primitive people. The novel was published a decade before the United States began asserting itself as a world power in the Spanish-American War, which led, as we noted earlier, to Twain's declaration in 1900 that he was an "anti-imperialist." But because we read it after the "American Century," it's possible to see Hank's use of superior technology to impose his will on a "native" population as a quest for power rather than an act of liberation.

And as soon as it seems possible to read *Connecticut Yankee* ironically, as an unreliable first-person narrative, the novel begins rewriting itself in profound ways. Hank, for example, sees himself as "the champion of hard, unsentimental, common-sense and reason" (384), as the antithesis to the irrational, superstitious, credulous minds of the Arthurians. His own words and actions, however, betray how uncritically, how superstitiously he believes in the values of the culture he comes from. One of the many ironies that pile up concerns cleanliness, that perennial American preoccupation. Hank never gets over his astonishment at the way Arthurians don't bathe, don't see cleanliness as next to godliness, don't even realize how dirty they are. The plot comes back to this difference many times, but most pointedly when Hank introduces soap into the kingdom, and then sends the knights across the land (something like subscription agents with a book) to sell the populace on the idea of washing, even if they have to use force. Here is how Hank describes the success of this "reform," as he calls it, on the factory he builds in the castle at Camelot:

> My soap factory felt the strain early. At first I had only two hands; but before I had left home I was already employing fifteen, and running night and day; and the atmospheric result was getting so pronounced that the king went sort of fainting and gasping around and said he did not believe he could stand it much longer, and Sir Launcelot got so that he did hardly anything but walk up and down the roof and swear, although I told him it was worse up there than anywhere else. (140)

Just as the people of the sixth century take the dirt on their bodies for granted, so Hank (who falls into Camelot from his factory job in nineteenth-century Hartford) takes industrial air pollution as a fact of life and a sign of progress – both are oblivious to what seems monstrous to the other. For the reader, though, it's hard to see any real improvement – the filth is either on the bodies or in the air – while what stands out most clearly is how both Hank and the Arthurians are trapped inside their "inherited ideas" (65).

While Huck remains blind to the way his perceptions of race and slavery are deformed by his ideological preconceptions, Hank does realize the power of cultural conditioning. In fact, it is in Hank's voice that Twain first discusses this theme overtly. What Hank calls "training" becomes one of the main themes of Twain's work during the last two decades of his life. As a mysterious stranger from a radically different culture, Hank is always aware of how historically contingent and culturally constructed are the beliefs and behaviors that the Arthurians assume are right and natural, eternal and real: their unquestioning acceptance of injustices like hereditary rank and chattel slavery convince Hank that "training is everything; training is all there is to a person. . . . We have no thoughts of our own, no opinions of our own" (162). His use of "we" is not merely rhetorical: he acknowledges that his own "inherited ideas" flow in the paths laid down by his own training, "in ruts worn deep by time and habit" (65). But he makes a fundamental distinction between the shams and delusions that pass as truth in the 6th century, and the enlightened values he brings with him from 19th century America. To him, for example, it is unquestionably a great reform when, after he defeats chivalry in the lists, the Round Table is used "for business purposes" as a stock exchange, where seats, including the Siege Perilous that had been set apart for the morally pure Galahad, are sold for money (400). Believing in capitalism the way the knights believe in chivalry and nobility, Hank thinks of money as a sacrament: one of his first reforms is to have the kingdom "adopt the American values exclusively," and he puts his pennies and nickels and dimes into circulation as "new blood" that will "freshen up its life" (119). The consequences of Hank's "reforms," however, often provide reasons to re-examine the assumptions on which they are based: in Twain's re-writing of the Camelot legend, it is not Launcelot's adulterous relationship with Guenever that precipitates the catastrophe but rather his unethical manipulations of the stock market. With details like this, the story that Twain began as a cold, hard look at feudal Europe seems instead to be holding up a fun-house mirror to his own late-19th century America, and the narrative apparently opens up an increasingly ironic gap between its narrator and its meaning.

By the end it could be argued that that gap becomes a chasm which swallows up the narrative itself. One of Hank's most fundamental faiths is in technological progress. His first act as Arthur's new minister is to set up a patent office, which amounts to the cathedral of his belief that machines, "all the thousand willing and handy servants of steam and electricity" (397), are what will make the world a better place. He sees new inventions as saviors, and calls the great inventors – "Gutenberg, Watt, Arkwright, Whitney, Morse, Stephenson, Bell" – "the creators of this world – after God" (323). On the other hand, the story continues to turn out ironies like the soap factory that produces dirt. Near the beginning, for example, in the chapter called "Beginnings of Civilization," Hank uses a surprising metaphor to express the industrial democracy he is secretly preparing to spring upon the 6th century: although hidden, it is "as substantial a fact as any serene volcano, standing innocent with its smokeless summit in the blue sky and giving no sign of the rising hell in its bowels" (82). At this early stage, there is nothing in the narrative to which a reader can attach the suggestion that the 19th century light with which Hank plans to illuminate the Dark Ages is infernal. In the middle of the novel, however, are five chapters set in the Valley of Holiness, where Hank restores the fountain. Hank has technicians working in secret to lay down telephone lines throughout the kingdom, and he is delighted to find they've already wired the Valley. He is especially delighted that they have set up the phone in a cave formerly occupied by one of the hermits that the Arthurians worship as saints and that Hank scorns as unwashed humbugs:

> Now what a radical reversal of things this was; what a jumbling to-gether of extravagant incongruities, what a fantastic conjunction of opposites and irreconcilables – the home of the bogus miracle become the home of a real one, the den of a medieval hermit turned into a telephone office! (229)

We can hear in Hank's use of the word "miracle" how devoutly he believes in this new technology, although when he makes a call to Camelot, the text gives us an occasion to doubt. Back in Camelot they have been told about Hank's restoration of the fountain, but accord-ing to what they heard, that occurred in a very different place than the Valley of Holiness.

> "What was the name, then?" [Hank asks into the phone.]
>   "The Valley of Hellishness" [is the reply from Camelot].
>   "That explains it. Confound a telephone, anyway. It is the very demon"
> [for mixing up sounds] (230)

These suggestions, that there is something potentially hellish about the technology that Hank believes in as the means to a happier fu-ture, erupt into the machine-made holocaust of the ending. Inside Merlin's Cave, Hank and his technicians turn a dynamo into a weapon of mass destruction which, in the final battle between him and the Arthurians, gives him the means to kill 25,000 knights. When Hank first wakes up in the 6th century, he finds himself "under an oak tree, on the grass, with a whole beautiful and broad country landscape all to myself" (5). When at the end he looks over the world wrought by his electricity and dynamite and gattling guns, we may remember the phrase "Valley of Hellishness": "we could not count the dead, because they did not exist as individuals, but merely as homogeneous proto-plasm, with alloys of iron and buttons" (432); "of course there was a smell of burning flesh" (437); "*There* was a groan you could *hear!*" (440). According to the Camelot legend, the story has to end with a tragic, apocalyptic final battle, but the ending Twain writes for his version also looks forward to the destructiveness of 20th century warfare. "Our camp was enclosed with a solid wall of the dead" (439) – in the face of such evidence Hank's blind allegiance to technology seems as superstitious as the Arthurians' belief in magic, and a lot more dangerous. Hank never doubts that his machine gods can set humankind free, but in the last chapter of his story, written by his assistant Clarence, we can see how people can become imprisoned by the machines they create: "We were in a trap, you see," writes Clarence, "a trap of our own making" (443). We may also remember the soap factory Hank was so proud of when we note the final by-product of his killing-machine, because what kills Hank's forces is air pollution: "I was among the first," Clarence admits, "made sick by the poisonous air bred by those dead thousands" (443).

Nor does it occur to Hank to question whether his 19th-century doctrine of "progress" might be just as irrational as the medieval idea of "the divine right of kings," but the high-tech bang that brings the story of his project to reconstruct the 6th century to one of the most apocalyptic climaxes in literature certainly rocks the pedestal on which that ideal rests. It seems impossible that any reader of *Connecticut Yankee* could fail to be disturbed by the violence of its ending, but in fact no contemporary American reviewer even mentioned it. Interpreting silence is tricky, but perhaps in what they didn't say about the book those reviewers reveal what they were unwilling to see. The acknowledged cultural credo of late-19th-century America was defined by the beliefs Hank embodies: in business opportunities and venture capitalism, and in invention and technology, marching toward a better future under the banner of progress. As the late-19th century became the *fin de siècle*, however, a counter-narrative gained credibility. Best articulated by Henry Adams' autobiography, *The Education of Henry Adams* (1907), this line of thought traced the movement of history not as a steady rise from darkness toward the light but as a fall toward a modernity experienced as loss, complexity and futility. One of Adams' culminating chapters is called "The Virgin and the Dynamo," in which, like Twain's novel, he contrasts the human condition in medieval and modern times, but unambiguously to the advantage of the former: spirituality has given way to brute materialism, order to social, moral and intellectual chaos.

Adams was born in 1838, just three years after Sam Clemens. As cohorts, they lived through the same drastic transformations that remade American society over the course of the century. In a surreal way, the fantastic situation Twain contrives for the novel mirrors that national experience. The society Hank wakes up in is predominantly rural and agrarian, as America was in the 1840s. The new society he abruptly forces onto that land is the industrialized, urban America that Twain and his readers in 1889 found themselves living in. Some commentators have suggested that we can read *Connecticut Yankee* even more specifically as the fantastic re-enactment of the American Civil War. Rotate the novel's east–west polarity 90 degrees, and the fact that the agrarian culture Hank is transported to is also aristocratic and slave-owning identifies it as the South, while as a "Yankee" his values are those of the manufacturing, capitalist, abolitionist North. Hank can even be seen as a kind of carpet-bagger, whose attempt to "reconstruct" that "southern" society fails; in keeping with the novel's sense of going backwards in time, that failure then precipitates a destructive civil war. Hank mentions the American South and the Civil War overtly several times, and the landscape he describes, with its large manor houses and slave quarters, does look more like the ante bellum culture Huck moves through as the raft travels south than like any documentable medieval past. These associations are another way of establishing how subversively the narrative turns on itself, how deeply this journey to Europe takes us into the truth of the 19th century American experience. If they felt this as they read the book, those contemporary critics could not have mentioned the ending at all without acknowledging that change might be destructive rather than progressive, that the future their wonderful new machines were building for them might be far less inhabitable than the past that they had lost. "The Tale of the Lost Land" – that is the surprising title of Hank's first-person story. It not only evokes the nostalgia in which *Tom Sawyer* wraps the pre-industrial past; it can give us another way of appreciating why Americans trapped in the modernity Hank celebrates as utopian but nonetheless keeps associating with "hellishness" would turn so gladly to the simpler world of St Petersburg.

Twain also had personal reasons for doubting his own faiths in technology and commerce. He loved the new inventions of his era. In 1876, for example, he became the first person to install a telephone in his home (and so had plenty of chances to learn firsthand about garbled messages), and several years later became the first author to have a manuscript typed on one of Remington's just-invented machines. He took out several patents himself, including one for a self-pasting scrapbook that made more money for him than any other book. As Justin Kaplan points out, for Twain the writing of *Connecticut Yankee* was connected to one machine in particular: the typesetting machine being developed by an inventor named James W. Paige.[12] Twain's relationship to this machine began in 1881, with a $5,000 investment. In 1886, at almost exactly the same moment that he began writing the novel, believing that there were millions of dollars of profit to be had from it, he organized a company to perfect and market the machine. By 1887 he had given Paige over $50,000, and the monthly costs of the project were a serious drain on Twain's wealth. At the same time, the other company he had founded, the publishing company that brought out *Huck Finn* in 1885, was having severe cashflow problems too. It scored great hits with both Huck's book and Ulysses Grant's *Memoirs* (1885–86), but when, carried away with those successes, Twain kept adding less profitable books to the company's list, and especially once he began drawing money from the company to underwrite Paige's work on the machine, the publishing company became a liability too. The end did not come until 1894, when after costing Twain over $200,000, the machine's final failure forced the publishing company into bankruptcy, leaving the author himself over $100,000 in debt. But by 1888 Twain's ill-conceived investments forced him to put his imagination back to work.

As we noted in the last chapter, he had hoped that his publishing company and the typesetting machine would enable him to retire as a public author. He told Mrs. Fairbanks in 1886 that his Arthurian story "is to be my holiday amusement for six days every summer the rest of my life. Of course I do not expect to publish it; nor indeed any other book."[13] But by the summer of 1887 it was already clear that the only way to get the machine the money it needed was for the publishing company to bring out a new book by Mark Twain. It was under these circumstances that he wrote most of the novel. Like Hank, Twain's conscious faith in the gods of capitalism and technology did not waver. He planned, for example, to complete writing the novel "the /[same] day the machine finishes."[14] In a letter to Howells in 1889, going over some last minute details about *Connecticut Yankee*, he sounds exactly like Hank when he invites Howells to visit Hartford to see the typesetter work: "Come & see this sublime magician of iron & steel work his enchantments."[15] At the same time, as machine and company kept making greater demands on him, his unconscious doubts about his own progress and his unacknowleged anxieties about his own future may have led his imagination toward the darkness of the end of *Connecticut Yankee*, where Hank's business schemes and new machines destroy just about everything.

Hank's story also suggests why Twain would have wanted to retire from authorship after publishing *Huck Finn*. Despite all the similarities I've noted between Hank and Huck as narrative vantage points, when it comes to his dominant character trait he is much more like Tom Sawyer. As much as Tom, or as much as "Mark Twain," Hank craves attention. "I so wanted to gather-in that great triumph," Hank says about his plan to use the eclipse to convince Camelot he is a mighty wizard, "and be the centre of all the nation's wonder and reverence" (45). More than money or even political power, what Hank wants most is "to be so celebrated and such a centre of homage" (55). And like Tom, to get and keep the attention of his Arthurian audience he puts on shows compulsively and with great virtuosity. He is a master of show-biz effects. At the eclipse he knows just how to strike a theatrical pose: "I was in one of the most grand attitudes I ever struck" (47). Even in a private conversation he modulates his voice "by dramatically graded stages, to my colossal climax, which I delivered in as sublime and noble a way as I ever did such a thing in my life" (41–2). As opposed to his enthusiasm for machinery and money, this "circus-side of [his] nature" (114) is hardly consistent with his job as a factory foreman, nor is the "most loathed" joke that Hank claims to have "heard oftenest" – the one about the "humorous lecturer" and an "ignorant audience" – the kind of joke men tell each other in factories (76–7). Instead, the novel's preoccupation with performing for audiences derives directly from Twain's career as a celebrity. Twain's failure to maintain a distinction between Hank as a created persona and his own feelings and experience can be seen whenever Hank puts on a show. When he announces the "miracle" he'll perform to restore the fountain, for example, he says his "idea was, doors open at 10:30, performance to begin at 11:25" – despite the fact that in the sixth century there are no clocks, nor even, since the show is outside, any doors to open (220). "Doors open at 7:30, the trouble will begin at 8" – that's the signature slogan with which "Mark Twain" advertised his lectures, and just as that line gets taken from Twain's act and projected onto Hank's, so throughout the novel Twain uses Hank's adventures among the Arthurians to dramatize his own ambitions and frustrations as a claimant for America's popular favor.

Although Hank mentions his inventions, schools, factories and other reforms, we never actually see him invent anything – except a public image. The novel's central scenes are almost all scenes of performance: the eclipse, Merlin's tower, the restoration of the fountain, the knights on bicycles, the joust with Sir Sagramore. In these scenes the people of the sixth century play the part of the mass audience: "the seated multitudes" at the eclipse, for example, "rose rank above rank, forming sloping terraces that were rich with color" (45). The part Hank plays is defined by the appetites and expectations of that audience: he is Sir Boss, a mightier wizard than even Merlin. He is forced into that role in the first show he puts on, when, stripped naked and bound to the stake, the only way he can save himself is by pretending to have the magical power to destroy everyone else. "I was a new man!" he says, when the sun goes into eclipse and Hank's star is born (47). This "new man," however, is an impostor. Like mysterious strangers, frauds and impostors are characters Twain's imagination keeps recurring to. *Connecticut Yankee* can help us understand the connection between the two types. The only way a mysterious stranger like Hank can create a receptive place for himself among people whose assumptions and beliefs he does not share is as an impostor.

But while Sir Boss becomes one of the greatest figures in Arthurian England, his image is entirely at odds with everything Hank Morgan himself claims to stand for. Hank despises Merlin and magic, and yet to the audiences who watch him "make three passes in the air" with his hands at Merlin's tower (59), or who hear him pronounce the dread names of evil spirits "with a kind of awfulness which caused hundreds to tremble, and many women to faint" at the fountain (221), Sir Boss is simply a better magician than Merlin. Indeed, to produce the effect he seeks at the joust with Sagramore, Hank's performance is careful to make it seem as if the magic spell of invisibility that Merlin weaves around the knight actually works. His written description of Merlin's efforts is full of scornful humor: Merlin "cast a dainty web of gossamer threads over Sir Sagramore which turned him into Hamlet's ghost"; but in the show he puts on for the audience that packs the grandstand he "cock[s] my ear . . . as if noting the invisible knight's position and progress by hearing, not sight" (386).

While Hank is the radical enemy of superstition and "the frivolous black arts," the show Sir Boss puts on can only reinforce the public's belief in magic. This contradiction between reformer and performer, Hank himself and his public persona, sets up the conflict that Hank remains trapped in throughout the novel. He is determined to destroy the power of the Church, but his greatest theatrical triumph is the "miracle" he enacts at the fountain, done on behalf of the Church. He takes Arthur through the kingdom in disguise as a commoner, and then as a slave, as part of his program eventually to abolish both slavery and aristocratic rank. That journey climaxes, however, when the knights pedal to the rescue on bikes, and Hank seizes the occasion for another brilliant piece of showmanship, shouting at the crowd:

> "On your knees, every rascal of you, and salute the king! Who fails shall sup in hell to-night!"
> I always use that high style when I'm climaxing an effect. . . . (380)

Hank gloats over the way this moves the crowd – "It was fine to see that astonished multitude go down on its knees." It doesn't seem to occur to him that this "effect," depending on the power of words like "king" and "hell," moves the crowd in exactly the opposite direction from the one in which, as the apostle of democracy and rational thought, he set out to lead them.

There is a huge disparity between the story Hank thinks he is telling and the drama he actually enacts. To him, his is the story of the superior man working heroically to emancipate "an ignorant race" (219) with the truth he brings from another world. That story, though, remains essentially offstage. In the scenes that the novel shows us, which happen onstage in every respect, we witness Hank instead allowing this society's prejudices to re-create him. As a prophet he can try to have an effect on society, or as a popular entertainer he can produce an effect on an audience – but these projects are mutually exclusive. Here we should recall the original occasion for that journal entry that became the seed of *Connecticut Yankee*: Twain's lecture tour performing and promoting *Huck Finn*. He not only read Malory's book on that tour; he and Cable took to calling their manager "Sir Sagramore le Desirous" and, as he wrote Livy, "us[ing] the quaint language of the book in the [railroad] cars & hotels."[16] At exactly this time he was appearing nightly in front of American audiences as "Mark Twain" and delighting them with the Evasion episode from *Huck Finn*, which like Hank's performances as Sir Boss gave the audiences what they were looking for but betrayed the truth the performer believed. It is possible, in other words, to see the false self Hank creates to impress the 6th century as Clemens' imaginative way of expressing his own estrangement from and frustration with the show he has been putting on as "Mark Twain." Hank's public success becomes at the same time the measure of his failure, and it's even possible that out of this bind (like being trapped in a suit of armor keeps you from getting in touch with yourself) comes the violent rage that fuels *Connecticut Yankee's* apocalyptic ending. For all Hank's performances are saturated with hints of violence: the pose he strikes at the eclipse, for example, is of someone who can destroy the whole world; when he sets off the fireworks at the fountain, not only do women faint, but "lots of people shrieked" and "moan and howl," while "foundlings collapsed by platoons" (221). Long before the final battle, in other words, Hank has been metaphorically knocking his audience dead. Yet despite his hostile contempt for the Arthurians, he cannot escape his dependence on their attention as the source of his greatness. When he literally knocks 'em dead at the end, he also defeats himself.

Looked at this way, in the context of the performances of "Mark Twain," Hank's final "entertainment" (he actually uses that word, as well as "performance," to describe the climactic battle, 436 and 423) becomes even more destructive. Like Tom Sawyer's ultimate act of heroism, it happens in a cave. There are even 52 boys present as Hank's "army," boys just about Tom and Huck's age. To perfect his killing machine, Hank "creat[es] a river a hundred feet wide" (440). Boys, a cave, a river – these are the ingredients out of which Twain had made his best beloved novels. Now, however, thousands of knights (trapped in *their* armor) drown in the river, and all the boys die in the cave. In the very last chapter, waking up from the enchanted sleep into which Merlin, getting the last laugh, has cast him, Hank finds himself once more in the 19th century, but now he is nostalgic for the 6th. The whole time he was there, of course, he wanted to turn it into the 19th, but now, he says, it's that past that contains "all that could make life worth the living" (447). On the book's last page he dies, in delirium: the "dream" with which that comic journal entry started ends with Hank's "hideous dreams," in which both worlds, the past he destroyed but now longs for and the present to which he has returned "as a stranger and forlorn," are equally unreal to him. It is a bizarre and somehow perfect note to strike at the end of this novel in which so many things cancel each other out. The book's realistic attack on the past is undone by the surreal way in which it reveals the terrors of modernity, leaving no place of refuge. The novel added to Twain's stature as an American favorite while exposing acceptance by an audience as potentially the most devasting form of self-betrayal. *Which Was the Dream?* – that is the title of one of the late, unfinished fictions in which Twain kept obsessively returning, without getting anywhere, to the question of his own career, trying to sort out the achievements, regrets and estrangements with which it had left him. Although it can be read simply for its humor, *Connecticut Yankee* is the first full-scale expression of that confusion. By the time Twain finished it, it was already hard to tell what isn't a nightmare.

Looking for Refuge
Pudd'nhead Wilson and "Hadleyburg"

Mark twain. These are the two words Sam Clemens chose to give a name to his public persona, first as a writer, then as a lecturer, ultimately as one of the most celebrated personages on the planet. There is some dispute about what he had in mind when he first used "Mark Twain" as a byline in 1863. Most scholars accept the explanation he invariably provided: that he took the term directly from his experience as a riverboat pilot for whom it meant "two fathoms," or 12 feet of water under the boat. The alternative explanation, preferred more or less seriously by some scholars who would rather identify Twain with the frontier West than the Mississippi Valley, adds a meaning derived from the bohemian life he led as a Nevada newspaper reporter: "mark twain" was supposedly the order he gave the bartenders in Virginia City saloons, where he was usually so thirsty that he wanted two drinks, and so broke that they both had to be marked down on his tab. Either way, whether fathoms or drinks, "mark twain" literally means "note two." It might be mere coincidence that someone born Clemens wrote so often about claimants; his novel *The American Claimant* (1892) is about an aspirant to a British earldom, and characters like Tom Sawyer, Hank Morgan, and David Wilson are all claimants for popular attention and status. But it is surely significant that the person who chose Twain as his pseudonym was also fascinated by twins.

Sam Clemens had one older and one younger brother, but no twin. The writings of Mark Twain, on the other hand, display an ongoing preoccupation with various forms of twinship. His imagination kept returning, for example, to the figure of the "Siamese twin," the common term in his time for conjoined twins. *The Prince and The Pauper* are not related, but resemble each other so exactly that when they switch clothes not even their parents recognize any difference. Huck Finn and Tom Sawyer – Huck Sawyer and Tom Finn? – are also twinned, linked so closely in most readers' minds that it is hard to think of one without the other, and so closely in Twain's imagination that, as we said, Huck almost steals Tom's story and, at the end of Huck's, Tom winds up taking over the narrative while Huck himself impersonates Tom. Another variant of this preoccupation is the conflicted twaining of a self that we noted in the last chapter: Hank Morgan and Sir Boss are the private and public identities of the same person, but on the basis of their beliefs and behavior they are deeply at odds with each other. In his sketch "The Facts Concerning the Recent Carnival of Crime in Connecticut" (1876) Twain describes his conscience as a deformed, dwarfed twin that lives inside the self but incessantly strives against its happiness. He read Robert Louis Stevenson's *Dr. Jekyll and Mr. Hyde* (1886) with great interest in its dramatization of a double self; his last remarks, as he lay on his deathbed in 1910, were about "one of his old subjects, Dual Personality," "Jeckyll and Hyde phases in literature and fact."[1] It was a subject he knew firsthand.

By the last two decades of Sam Clemens' career as Mark Twain, his private and public selves were poles apart. Publically, "Mark Twain" was internationally beloved by millions of readers who were ready to laugh as soon as they heard his name. The world showed its appreciation in a number of unmistakable ways. To pay his debtors after his bankruptcy in 1894, for instance, he arranged an around the world lecture tour that took him, during 1895–1896, across the northwestern United States, and then across the British Empire – Australia, New Zealand, India and South Africa. Everywhere he went, the theaters were packed with delighted audiences. His literary achievement was confirmed by three honorary doctorates: in 1901 from Yale, in 1902 from Missouri, and, as the capstone, in 1907 from Oxford, which Twain, like most Americans, considered the world's foremost university – he had repeatedly attacked the idea of Europe's cultural superiority but never exorcised it. To receive the Missouri degree he went back in person one last time to Hannibal and the River, and his reception there by the admiring crowds would have matched even Tom Sawyer's grandiose expectations. Twain spent most of the 1890s living in Europe to economize, but after he moved back to America in 1900 he became one of the social world's favorite guests at banquets, including several grand ones that were held to honor him. The mass media of the time – newspapers and magazines – kept his name and remarks steadily in the public eye, and made him one of the world's most frequently photographed people; they knew his humorous sayings made great copy, and his features were very photogenic. Although he didn't begin wearing the white suit until the end of 1906, it soon became as much a part of his image as the mustache, the mane of white hair, the twinkling blue eyes and the cigar. To his contemporararies he was an ideal American self, the biggest star in the heaven of popular success.

Twain himself once said, though, that "Every man is a moon, and has a dark side which he never shows to anybody."[2] Twain kept this other self offstage and out of print; summing up his life at his 70th birthday dinner, for example, he joked about drinking and smoking, not about "the damned human race." In private, however, he wrote hundreds of pages of novels he was unable to finish, surreal fantasies of catastrophes and futility: ships and houses destroyed in fire, families shrunk to microscopic size doing battle with huge germs, the universe as the bloodstream of an alcoholic tramp. Travel is a persistent motif in these late, unpublishable fictions, but the journeys end in places like "The Great Dark," where people drift helplessly in an eternal calm.[3] When revisionist critics like Waldo Frank and Van Wyck Brooks began exploring Twain's dark side in the years after World War I, people who wanted to hold on to the idol of "Mark Twain" as a humorist for whom the American dream of making it had come true either denied his late anger and despair or fell back on the belief that his pessimism was the result of personal traumas.[4] He certainly suffered terrible losses. His oldest daughter, Susy, died in August 1896, alone in Hartford, just weeks after Twain reached England at the end of that lecture tour that had taken him all the way around the world and a long way toward financial solvency. Susy was his favorite daughter, and he blamed himself for her death, but her loss was even more devastating to Livy, whose own fragile health began seriously to fail as a result. Much of her last years were spent on a sick bed from which her husband was ordered kept away by doctors who felt Twain's presence exascerbated her illness. His daughter Jean's epilepsy also deteriorated after Susy's death, and after Livy died in 1904 both Jean and Clara, his remaining daughters, felt estranged from him most of the time. Yet the bitterness is already there in his work before any of these griefs were visited upon him. In this last chapter we'll look closely at his last two major fictions – *The Tragedy of Pudd'nhead Wilson* (1894) and "The Man That Corrupted Hadleyburg" (1899): ironic un-writings of popular success and humorous performance, those twinned motifs at the center of the career "Mark Twain."

According to Twain's account, the origin of *Pudd'nhead Wilson* was a picture he saw of the Tocci twins, a " 'freak' – or 'freaks' "[5] who toured America in the early 1890's much as Chang and Eng, the original "Siamese twins," had exhibited themselves during the 1830s. Two heads and four arms conjoined in one body, this pair was intended to be the occasion for a farce that Twain decided to set in an ante bellum village on the Missouri side of the Mississippi River – in other words, he was going back again to the landscape of his childhood, this time in the company of a "freak," a very mysterious stranger. As he was writing it, he said, "it changed itself from a farce to a tragedy" (229), but he published most of the completed portions of the original design as *The Comedy of Those Extraordinary Twins*, which was included in American editions of *Pudd'nhead Wilson*. In this sketch the comedy plays out along the lines of his much earlier "Personal Habits of the Siamese Twins" (1869). Although in fact both Chang and Eng and the Toccis, Giocanni and Giacomo, agreed on most things and "live[d] on excellent terms with each other,"[6] in both his sketches Twain defines each twin as the antithesis of the other. In *Those Extraordinary Twins*, for example, Angelo is a very devout tea-totaler while Luigi is a hard-drinking free-thinker. The slight plot of the original farce initially focuses on the village's amazed reception of these strange newcomers, and then mainly on the twins' inescapable dilemma, the persistent difficulties of sharing a body with someone whose appetites, values, ambitions and temperament are radically different.

It obviously increases the potential comedy in the situation to make the twins so diametrically dissimilar, especially when it's the temperance-preaching teatotaler who gets drunk whenever his brother has a whisky. At the same time, the way Twain kept recurring to this figure suggests that under the comedy was a serious concern with the nature of identity or selfhood. Twain may actually have met Sigmund Freud in 1898, during the year he lived in Vienna,[7] but could not even have heard of Freud's theories of the unconscious in the 1890s, for it wasn't until the 20th century began that Freud began publishing his theoretical maps of the human psyche. Within the unsophisticated terms that were available in those pre-Freudian days, however, Twain seems to be using the "extraordinary twins" to explore and dramatize the reality of psychic conflict along lines that often parallel psychoanalytic thought. From this point of view his decision to stage such a dramatization on that charged Freudian terrain, the scene of his own childhood, becomes very suggestive. But exactly what he might be trying to suggest about the mysteries of his own ambivalences remains a mystery itself, for Twain's imagination – working, he claimed, against his conscious will – disrupted the story he was writing with another narrative. At the center of that new story is not a united-divided self, but pair of changelings, two infants whose identities are switched. And with this change Twain's focus also changes, from what could be called the psychological to the sociological, from "dual personality" to a society divided by race and caste.

The tragedy that displaced the farce begins with three new arrivals in the village: a young man named David Wilson "wander[s]" into town "from his birthplace in the interior of the State of New York" (58), and two babies are born in the house of Percy Northumberland Driscoll, one of the town's leading white citizens. Both babies are "white" to look at, but only one, Driscoll's son Tom, is "white" legally and socially. The other is the son of another leading white citizen, but born out of wedlock to a slave named Roxy, and so legally "black" and enslaved. When Mrs. Percy Driscoll dies less than a week later, the task of raising both children devolves on Roxy. When the infants are seven months old, Percy Driscoll threatens to sell all his slaves "DOWN THE RIVER" for a minor offense; although this doesn't happen, Roxy is so horrified at the possibility that her child might meet such a fate that that night, in a complex and moving scene that begins with her intention to drown both her child and herself in the river, Roxy decides to switch the two babies and so free her son from slavery.

In a number of ways this resembles the plot Twain had used in *The Prince and The Pauper*, where Tom Canty, a beggar from Offal Court, and Edward, son of Henry VIII and heir to the British throne, change places; in both cases a character called Tom is promoted from the lowest class to the highest, and in both stories the switch is made by an exchange of clothes. But Twain's account of this breach of the color line takes a very different turn than his earlier fable about inverting the hierarchy of class. Like *A Connecticut Yankee in King Arthur's Court*, written several years later, Twain's novel about Tudor England has a very egalitarian emphasis. Tom Canty makes a good prince, in both senses: he acts with so much natural grace and intelligence that his retainers never suspect he is an impostor, and as prince his acts reveal him to be "kind and gentle, and a sturdy and determined champion of all that were oppressed."[8] And Edward's experiences while trapped inside the identity of the pauper, like Hank's travels through Arthur's realm, allow both him and Twain's readers to see the injustices of an aristocratic system from below. But while that novel dramatizes the arbitrariness of caste distinctions – outside of their clothes Tom and Edward are equals – it is much harder to say what point *Pudd'nhead Wilson* is making about race and slavery.

In the identity of Tom Driscoll, Roxy's son does not make a good master. He is a coward and a bully who grows up to become a liar, a gambler, a thief and eventually a murderer. The narrative offers two contradictory explanations for his bad behavior. Its cause may be his nurture, what in other works Twain would call his "training." "'Tom' was a bad baby," the narrator says, "from the very beginning of his usurpation" (75); an implication here is that the kind of conditioning he received as heir to the master's role in the slave-owning society warped his character. We're told that as a slave Roxy was forbidden to discipline the "white" child, and in a sequence of sentences it is clearly suggested that Tom's personality is the product of this environmental conditioning: "Tom got all the petting . . . In consequence Tom was a sicky child . . . Tom was 'fractious,' as Roxy called it, and overbearing . . ." (77). On the other hand, his bad behavior may be innate, genetic. Twice, for instance, the narrator uses forms of the word "nature" – the familiar antithesis of "nurture" – in his diagnoses of Tom's immorality: "Tom did his humble comrade these various ill turns partly out of native viciousness . . ." (79); Roxy becomes the "victim of [Tom's] capricious temper and vicious nature" (81). Given America's long-standing anxieties about race, the potential stakes are quite large here: is Tom such a "vicious" person because, though you can take the slave out of the cradle, you cannot take his immoral "nature" out of the slave? or, is Tom's corrupt life the result of the deformed, unjust slave-owning social system that makes victims of everyone? Because of both the controversy about *Huckleberry Finn*'s treatment of race and the way *Pudd'nhead Wilson* puts race and slavery right at the center of its story, the later novel is being more frequently taught these days. But as with *Huck Finn*, it would be a gross simplification to say that *Pudd'nhead Wilson* is unambiguously either racist or anti-racist.

At the outset it seems to take a position that is far closer to our 21st-century assumptions than most thinking about race in Twain's own times. The scene in which Roxy's character is introduced does a brilliant job of exposing how racial prejudice works, and how far from nature and reality are the socially constructed categories of "white" and "black." Before we see Roxy, we hear her. Our perspective is that of Pudd'nhead Wilson, as he sits indoors and through an open window overhears her conversation with another slave. We hear her dialect – "Fust-rate; how does *you* come on, Jasper?" is her first line – and we even hear her "care-free laughter" (63). Both the non-standard English and the sound of laughter are part of the stereotypical set of associations Twain's readers would have with black characters, and the narrative gives enough of her conversation to allow that pre-conceived image to form in those readers' minds. But when Wilson goes to the window to see her with his own eyes, that image is destroyed: "From Roxy's manner of speech a stranger would have expected her to be black, but she was not" (63). The result of four generations of miscegenation, Roxy is only "one sixteenth" "black." Though that percentage makes her legally a "negro" and "a slave, and saleable as such," the narrator does not hesitate, as Wilson and the reader see her this first time, to use the vocabulary usually reserved for white heroines to describe her: "She was of majestic form and stature; her attitudes were imposing and statuesque, and her gestures and movements distinguished by a noble and stately grace. . . . Her face was shapely, intelligent, and comely" (64). When the narrator goes on at the end of this description to note that, while Roxy is "as white as anybody," her son ("thirty-one parts white") is nonetheless "a slave and, by a fiction of law and custom, a negro," the narrative seems to be saying once and for all that "race" is merely a social convention, "a fiction" that culture creates and imposes on people the way Tom Sawyer, for example, tries to impose the unreal world of literary romance onto the landscape of middle America.

Opposed to this view, however, is the concept of "black blood," the idea that race is genetically transmitted rather than socially invented.

The characters themselves think of race this way. Looking again at Roxy two chapters and fifteen years after his first view of her, "Wilson said to himself, 'The drop of black blood in her is supersititous' . . . " (83). Even Roxy, to bring this discussion back to the question of Tom's "viciousness," believes not only that there is such a thing as "black blood," but also that it is an inescapable taint: scolding her son for his cowardly refusal to fight a duel to defend his honor according to the code of the southern gentleman, she says: "It's de nigger in you, dat's what it is. Thirty-one parts o' you is white, en on'y one part nigger, en dat po' little one part is yo' *soul*. 'Tain't wuth savin'" (157). Of course, it is important to notice that both these assertions are made inside quotation marks, by characters in the novel and not by the novel's narrator. As with Huck's first-person narrative, these racist beliefs – blacks are superstitious, whites are superior – reflect the thinking of characters living inside the slave-holding South; Twain might intend their comments about "black blood" to tell us nothing about real racial difference, but instead about the way racism works. He is certainly showing how even someone like Roxy, victim of both the arbitrary assignment of "blackness" and the real fact of enslavement, has been conditioned to think in the biased terms of her environment. When Wilson, for example, compliments both babies in that first meeting as equally "handsome," Roxy replies that "one of 'em ain't on'y a nigger" – the same prejudice that made it so hard for Huck to see Jim as fully human here comes between a mother and her own child (65). One of the most moving moments in the scene where Roxy switches the babies comes when she looks at her child for the first time in "white" clothes, rather than the "coarse tow-linen shirt" that is the badge of slavery: suddenly she can see who is really there, apart from the shadow of black inferiority that has lain like a stain on her son: "her eyes began to widen with astonishment and admiration . . . 'I *never* knowed you was so lovely'" (71). Among all the passages Twain writes on the power of "training," these demonstrations of how thoroughly Roxy has internalized the prejudices of the caste that has exploited and dehumanized her are perhaps the most poignant.

The events that the story develops, however, do little to encourage the reader to hold on to the unconventional idea that race is only a socially constructed fiction. In one of the few scenes showing how the other changeling, Chambers, has been effected by his upbringing as a slave, we hear him struggling correctly to use and pronounce a poly-syllabic word – "dissenhurrit" (103); it was a commonplace of both minstrelsy and more polite literature to suggest a connection between skin color and the capacity for language as a sign of intelligence, but since *all* Chambers' ancestors were "white," his thick dialect subverts that stereotypical linkage. Yet in *Pudd'nhead Wilson*, unlike *The Prince and the Pauper*, there is no symmetry in the account of the two changelings. The narrative keeps its focus almost entirely on Tom instead of Chambers, and shows Tom not simply failing to live up to the standards of the F.F.V. gentleman, but becoming a criminal presence that infests this village much like "Injun Joe" (another racially mixed figure) haunts St Petersburg. As a youth he murder-ously attacks Chambers with a knife; as a man, he actually sells his own mother down the river, and then goes on (using an "Indian knife" after having "blacked his face" [194]) to murder York Driscoll, his foster father, while cold-bloodedly robbing him. Tom's viciousness makes it impossible to sympathize with him, while at the same time the one character whom the novel does encourage readers to identify with, Pudd'nhead Wilson, becomes triumphant by laying down the color line with a vengeance in the dramatic scene with which the narrative climaxes.

Set in a courtroom at the end of a murder trial, that scene moves the novel generically toward the conventions of the detective story. Largely invented by Edgar Allan Poe in the 1840s, the genre was in vogue throughout the 1890s, mainly through the work of Arthur Conan Doyle, whose first Sherlock Holmes novel appeared in 1887. Even earlier Twain began trying to parody the genre, first in an unproduced play, then in a series of fictions that included *Tom Sawyer, Detective* (1896), one of the sequels in which he sought of capitalize on the popularity of his own books about Tom and Huck, and "A Double-Barreled Detective Story" (1902), in which Holmes himself appears in a burlesque role. While the town laughs at Wilson, how-ever, the narrator treats his ratiocinative intelligence and experiments with fingerprints with respect, and they, combined with a virtuoso command of theatrical technique, are what enable him to solve a mysterious murder and restore the violated social order by putting on a forensic show for the audience in the courtroom. By moving the story toward the mode of detective fiction, Twain shifts its focus from the white male as master to the white male as victim, and from the slave as victim to the freed "negro" as criminal. Using fingerprint evidence, Wilson is able not just to identify the person who used the knife to kill York Driscoll but also to re-establish the true identities of the babies whom Roxy switched, exposing Tom as both a murderer and an impostor, and also, to use the terms Wilson insists on at the climax of his courtroom speech, as "a negro and a slave" (222). The fingerprints don't establish race,[9] but they certainly give an air of scientific validity to the proceedings by which Wilson makes the distinction between "negro and slave" and "white and free" (222) a *fact* of law in this case. The white villagers, for whom the social status quo that Wilson restores depends on enslaving others, never question his unequivocal categorization of Tom as black. In the 1890s, slavery no longer existed, but there is evidence that Twain's contemporary white readers took the novel on the same terms Wilson lays down in court: that Tom is black, and inherently bad because he is black. The reviewer in the *Hartford Times* called him "the worthless Tom Driscoll, whose one-thirty-second part of 'nigger' blood proves, in spite of his octoroon mother's strong character, his bane and downfall."[10] The most striking evidence that Twain's contemporaries could read the novel without re-examining their racial preconceptions, however, is probably "Roxy Harvesting among the Kitchens," the illustration that Harper & Brothers, who became Twain's primary publishers in the 1890s, used for over thirty years as the novel's frontispiece (see Figure 7). The woman at the center of that drawing looks nothing like the character whom Twain describes in his text as "majestic," "noble," "stately" and "as white as anybody" (63–4). But she does look exactly like the "mammy/Aunt Jemima" stereotype that white American culture has long been so comfortable with as the archetypal image of the female slave. Twain's writing often points up how easy it is for people who have been ideologically trained to see what isn't there and to remain blind to what is; the fact that during the decades in which Harpers steadily reprinted this frontispiece no one, so far as I have been able to find out, ever raised any objections to it proves that point all too vividly.[11]

The abolition of slavery by no means resolved the complex issues that had gathered around the myth of "black blood." *Pudd'nhead Wilson* was published just two years before the Supreme Court, in *Plessy v Ferguson*, affirmed the constitutional legitimacy of the southern system of Jim Crow segregation, which made the kinds of racial calculations

ROXY HARVESTING AMONG THE KITCHENS

FIGURE 7   Frontispiece illustration by E. W. Kemble for *Pudd'nhead Wilson and Those Extraordinary Twins* (New York: Harper & Brothers, 1899)

that established "blackness" on the basis of one African American great-great-grandparent the law of the land for over half a century to come. Many of the defenders of the Jim Crow system argued that the safety of society depended on imposing severe restrictions on freed former slaves. In a widely disseminated essay, for example, Dr. Paul Barringer, Chairman of the Faculty at the University of Virginia, argued that Africans were inherently savage, that American slavery had actually improved the race by lifting them toward civilization, but that now, after emancipation, with the discipline of slavery removed "the young negro of the South . . . is reverting through hereditary forces to savagery."[12] The same racist thought – that the naturally vicious black population has to be kept in check by the whites – is the doctrine unashamedly and hysterically developed in Thomas Dixon's best-selling novels about Reconstruction, *The Leopard's Spots* (1902) and *The Clansman* (1905), which were the source for D. W. Griffith's phenomenally successful 1915 silent film, *The Birth of a Nation*. *Pudd'nhead Wilson* at no point argues that blacks must be kept down, and in fact quietly says in its second chapter that race itself is "a fiction" – but it nonetheless tells the story of a slave who is abruptly given freedom and becomes more and more immoral. By returning Tom to slavery, Wilson can be perceived as restoring peace and safety to the community that Tom had abused his privileges to prey upon.

Ironically, the narrator refers to Wilson's courtroom performance as the victorious end of "his long fight against hard luck and prejudice" (224). Wilson is a kind of changeling too: he goes from David to Pudd'nhead at the start, and then to popular hero at the end. Both these switches in his status result from public performances. On his first day in the village he tells a joke no one in his audience gets, and as a result of that failure becomes "a cipher in the estimation of the public" (87) for over twenty years, until his performance at the trial makes him a star. If at the climax Tom is exposed as the racial Other who is outcast from society, Wilson is simultaneously taken in by the community that had previously stigmatized him. Becoming a celebrity by putting on a show is of course one of the most pervasive motifs in the works of Mark Twain. Wilson's story links him with Hank Morgan, the outsider to Camelot who transforms himself into the celebrated "Sir Boss" through his performances, although its ending strikes the same note that Tom Sawyer's story ends on, with the successful showman at the center of an audience's admiring attention.

The narrator's laconic comment on this reversal in Wilson's reputation – "he was a made man for good" (224) – can be read ironically.
Two decades earlier, readers might remember, Wilson came to the
village from a world in which slavery did not exist. When he first saw
the two babies he was able to see them without any of the racial
prejudices that, for instance, blind even Roxy: he not only says "One's
just as handsome as the other," but also wonders how anyone could
"tell them apart . . . when they haven't any clothes on" (65). Referring to the same two children again in the courtroom, however,
Wilson now asserts that between them there is all the difference in
the world, or at least the one difference that matters most to this ante
bellum southern society: one is "a negro and a slave," the other is
"white and free" (222). They still look exactly the same as they did,
but what has changed is Wilson's way of perceiving: now he sees the
"whiteness" and "blackness," and the connection between these absolute racial distinctions and equally essentialized conditions of "freedom" and "slavery," that society tells him is there. His preconceptions
have been re-made by the village's prejudices; that may be how we're
supposed to read "a made man," and since those prejudices lead
people to deny the humanity of their own children, assimilating them
can hardly be "for good." Although the story it tells is of Wilson's rise
to popularity, the novel was published in America as *The Tragedy of
Pudd'nhead Wilson*. It is also possible that in telling the story of how
Wilson becomes a star through flattering the racial prejudices of his
audience, Twain is still trying to digest what he himself had done
with Jim and Huck's quest for freedom in *Huckleberry Finn*. The ritual
of labeling and casting out the black criminal may have been what
American culture wanted to see, in Wilson's time and in Twain's, but
as Twain knew, as the novel's opening chapters let us know he knew,
it wasn't the truth; it was a very self-serving fiction.

The village in *Those Extraordinary Twins* and *Pudd'nhead Wilson* is
called Dawson's Landing. It is the essentially same village that Clemens
grew up in and to which his imagination had already returned for
two other novels, though unlike Hannibal or St Petersburg, it is lo-
cated further south, "half a day's journey, per steamboat, below St
Louis" (55). "Down the river" are in fact the last words of *Pudd'nhead
Wilson* (226); if in *Huck Finn* that phrase at least included the possibility of freedom, as Huck and Jim head downriver on the raft, here it
defines the fate that not even Roxy's revolutionary action could alter;

despite the switch she made, her child ends up going down the river as a slave being punished. Most people get more nostalgic about their early lives as they get older, but each time Twain goes back to Hannibal his representation of the village makes it decidedly less attractive. In *Tom Sawyer* St Petersburg is a place we long to return to. In *Huck Finn*, it's the place the narrative is in flight from. In *Pudd'nhead Wilson*, Dawson's Landing is the place where characters get stuck, in a plot that feels as narrowly pre-determined as the thinking of the villagers. But although he kept going back to the time and place he grew up in, Twain never did finish coming to terms with it: among the many uncompleted projects of his last decades were his autobiography, which contains over a dozen inconsecutively written chapters on Hannibal, and "Schoolhouse Hill," a version of "The Mysterious Stranger" story set in St Petersburg. And he went back to Hannibal for the last major work of fiction he did finish and publish, the long short-story called "The Man That Corrupted Hadleyburg" (1899). The title is a bit misleading: no one corrupts Hadleyburg, because it was never sound or innocent to begin with; the man simply reveals the truth about what is already there. The punch-line of the bitter joke he springs on the village is that if you have the choice between "go[ing] to hell or Hadleyburg," you should "TRY AND MAKE IT THE FORMER."[13] This may recall the choice Huck was faced with, when trying to decide between letting St Petersburg know where Jim was and helping his friend himself; Huck heroically decides to "go to hell" too. In "Hadleyburg," however, there is no one to root for, and the clear sense that no one is going anywhere.

Once again the story revolves around a scene of public performance, but with a very suggestive difference. The performance is the work of another master showman, but this time he himself remains offstage and invisible while his script makes the audience the show. The "man," whose name we never learn, is described as a "mysterious big stranger" (*Collected Tales*, II: 391), and the show he stages is described as an act of revenge for some undefined "deep offense" that he has suffered from the town (*Collected Tales*, II: 426). Because "I could not kill you all," as he tells Hadleyburg in a letter, he comes up with a trap that will, before the watching eyes of the world, strip the village of the reputation for honesty that it wears as a false identity. The bait is also fake, another impostor: a bag of lead slugs that purports to be a fortune in gold coins. The show takes place in the town-hall and, like "the trouble" that "Mark Twain" advertised for his own public performances, begins "at eight" (*Collected Tales*, II: 392). The nineteen principal citizens who are caught in the trap are referred to as "claimants" for the sack (*Collected Tales*, II: 411). The scene in which they are systematically exposed as "frauds" (*Collected Tales*, II: 416) confounds the audience's expectations, but ultimately plays out as a humorous entertainment: "The house was in a roaring humor now, and ready to get all the fun out of the occasion that might be in it" (*Collected Tales*, II: 421).

"Against the assault of Laughter nothing can stand," Satan tells Twain's readers in "The Mysterious Stranger."[14] The stranger who exposes Hadleyburg is in part the kind of con man that Twain wrote about so often, and in part the kind of realist prophet that Twain as a writer aspired to be. At first the stranger's script strikes the town as "an adventure! Why, it's a romance; it's like the impossible things one reads about it books" (*Collected Tales*, II: 393–4). As the lies and frauds are systematically exposed, this adventure is un-written, and in its place is put "a stranger's eloquent recognition of what we are" (*Collected Tales*, II: 413). Although the stranger never does indicate how Hadleyburg had offended him, seen in the context of Twain's career as an entertainer Hadleyburg's performance can be read as the revenge of a humorist who has grown profoundly uneasy with his public role: instead of flattering the audience and their expectations, the show attacks and confounds them; instead of making himself ridiculous for their entertainment, the invisible showman gives them no one to laugh at *but themselves*. As in one of "Mark Twain"'s live performances, there is the continual sound of laughing, but if you listen closely, it's not hard to hear the note of apocalpytic menace in the hilarity:

> The pandemonium of delight which turned itself loose now was of a sort to make the judicious weep. Those whose withers were unwrung laughed till the tears ran down; the reporters, in throes of laughter, set down disordered pot-hooks which would never in the world be decipherable; and a sleeping dog jumped up, scared out of its wits, and barked itself crazy at the turmoil. (*Collected Tales*, II: 420)

In the end, the stranger goes away satisfied with his revenge, which seems pretty all-encompassing. The audience has been made to participate in what they wind up calling "a symbolical day!" (*Collected*

Tales, II: 421); "Pile up the Symbols!" they shout, and as one by one the town's nineteen leading citizens are exposed as frauds and hypocrites they often add "a grand and agonized and imposing 'A-a-a-a-men!'" (Collected Tales, II: 424) What they're left with after this anti-religious ceremony is finished – a pile of empty symbols that can only ironically gesture toward the value and meaning they were originally believed to embody – is very close to the littered landscape T. S. Eliot would call The Waste-Land (1922), on which so much Modernist literature is set. On the other hand, it's not clear how much really changes as a result of the stranger's visitation. It is tempting to read a lot into the town's decision to revise its motto, from "Lead us not into temptation" to "Lead us into temptation" (Collected Tales, II: 438). With that change, though the story doesn't call attention to this fact, they un-write perhaps the single most sacred text in Christian America, The Lord's Prayer from the New Testament. In terms of what Twain allowed himself to publish, this is without question his most radical realist revision of his culture's canonical texts. One other change could be portentious: like Samuel Clemens, Hadleyburg changes its name. But given the way the town goes back to its old ways – "It is an honest town once more," says the last sentence, apparently like Hadleyburg forgetting that its honesty was always only an illusion (Collected Tales, II: 438) – that new name seems to be merely another alias, a new false self, rather than a rebirth of any kind. Even the stranger's satisfaction is undermined by the fact that he too is ultimately taken in by the performance he staged: his belief that one citizen proves to be honest is erroneous.

"The Man That Corrupted Hadleyburg" is probably Twain's most perfectly organized fiction. As an example of his late work, perhaps its most striking feature is the way plot dominates character. What most readers associate with Twain are his memorable characters: Colonel Sellers in The Gilded Age, Tom Sawyer, Huck Finn, "Mark Twain" himself, each of whom seems to originate or at least dominate the story in which he appears. The nominal hero of "Hadleyburg" is named Edward Richards. He's one of the hypocritical "Nineteen," but since much of the tale is told from his point of view, the reader is tempted to invest him with more sympathy than the rest, and it is Richards who seems exceptional at the end: the one leading citizen who appears incorruptible to both the town and the stranger. But that apparent distinction, we know, is fraudulent, and even our readerly inclination to treat Richards as an individual is repeatedly challenged by the narrative's habit of pointing out how identically all nineteen leading families behave. "The discussions to-night [between Mr. and Mrs. Richards in their home, and Mr. and Mrs. Cox in theirs] were a sort of seeming plagiarisms of each other" (*Collected Tales*, II: 399); "All night long eighteen principal citizens did what their caste-brother Richards was doing at the same time" (*Collected Tales*, II: 409); and so on. The stranger's script makes all nineteen say the same line, just as the narrative treats them as essentially interchangeable: Wilson or Billson or Richards. This erasure of individuality also appears in *Pudd'nhead Wilson*: in chapter 1, for example, the people who pin the epithet on Wilson are referred to as "one," "another," "No. 3," "No. 4," "No. 5," and "No. 6." The other potential hero of "Hadleyburg," the extraordinary "stranger," remains completely anonymous, and by the end even his apparent exceptionality is undercut when the story's pervasive system of irony depicts him as another dupe conned by the show.

Behind this shrinkage of the individual can be seen the bleak determinist philosophy that Twain subscribed to at the end of his career. You can hear this belief in the anti-climax to which "Hadleyburg" brings the story of Richards' anti-heroism. He has a chance during the performance to stand up and admit that, like everyone else, he had succumbed to the temptation of that sack and so does not deserve the reward that the town and the stranger want to bestow on him, but he does not rise; the narrative registers his act, technically his not-acting, in its shortest paragraph:

> Edward fell – that is, he sat still; sat with a conscience which was not satisfied, but which was overpowered by circumstances. (*Collected Tales*, II: 428)

There's no potential for tragedy in this version of the "fall" as a sitting still, and no way to hold anyone responsible. The last word of this laconic paragraph is one that appears often in American texts from the final decades of Twain's life. "Under the circumstances," for example, is almost a refrain in Theodore Dreiser's *Sister Carrie*, published in the same year as "Hadleyburg." Dreiser's way of representing the larger forces that dwarfed the individual was to depict the lives of his characters in the setting defined by the huge cities of Chicago and

New York. The method of Twain's late fiction is to locate his characters in a structure of ironies that forestalled possibilities like the individual freedom Huck quests for or the social progress Hank works for
before they can even arise as possibilities. As an example, think of the
moment when Roxy apparently triumphs over the circumstance of
her exploitation as a slave. When Tom scorns her request for aid, she
forces him to beg her not to reveal the secret she knows about him.
The narrative presents the moment as the moral victory of a slave
over a master:

> The heir of two centuries of unatoned insult and outrage looked down
> on him and seemed to drink in deep draughts of satisfaction. Then she
> said:
>
> "Fine nice young white gen'l'man kneelin' down to a nigger-wench!
> I'se wanted to see dat jes once befo' I'se called." (109)

But Roxy's righteous pleasure depends on her having somehow
forgotten that Tom isn't "white," and that she herself put him in the
position of "gentleman" in the first place, so any victory she might
seem to win here is entirely fraudulent, and comes at the expense of
her own hopes. All the characters in "Hadleyburg" are constrained by
a similar set of ironies; the story's perfect structure is a measure of the
lack of individual possibilities in the fates of its characters.

Twain's determinism was undoubtedly influenced by growing
pessimisms of intellectuals and artists at the fin de siècle, but mainly
represented the end of the lines of thought he had been following on
his own for most of his career. He offered a quasi-systematic articu-
lation of his philosophy in one of his last books, *What Is Man?*,
published anonymously in 1906. A much shorter and more moving
expression of his views can be found in the very last work he published, a brief essay called "The Turning Point in My Life," which
appeared in *Harper's Bazaar* in February, 1910. In it he offers an
account of the process by which he came to be a writer. According to
him, he had nothing whatever to do with it. Instead, it was entirely
the result of "Circumstance" and "temperament," forces which take
the place of either divine providence or free will, and neither of
which is at all subject to an individual's control. "Circumstance," he
writes, "is man's master – and when Circumstance commands he
must obey" (*Collected Tales*, II: 932). How a man will respond to these

external commands depends on his "temperament" – and although that is an internal force, it too is beyond man's ability to direct or shape: temperament "is *born* in him, and he has no authority over it, neither is he responsible for its acts" (*Collected Tales*, II: 933). Looking back over the events of his life, he announces in a tone that sounds more like relief than resignation, more even like smugness than despair, "I was the author of none of them. Circumstance, working in harness with my temperament, created them all and compelled them all" (*Collected Tales*, II: 932). He is referring overtly to his actions, not his books, but it is still a very striking phrase for one of the world's most popular authors to use in an essay about "how I came to be literary" (*Collected Tales*, II: 931) – "I was the author of none of them." From the mysteries of his life – the ambiguous dream it had become, the guilts and regrets, even the phenomenal success – he took refuge in the thought that it had all been done *to* him, not *by* him. None of it, not even the adulation of the world, had been his fault.

When shortly after his death the authorship of *What Is Man?* became known, its idea that man was a meaningless machine shocked Twain's fans. To them he meant something very different. To them, for example, he was the entertaining apostle of individuality who in his "Seventieth Birthday Dinner Speech" taught, amongst the good-humored remarks about drinking and smoking, that "we can't reach old age by another man's road" and that "if you find you can't make seventy by any but an uncomfortable road, don't you go" (*Collected Tales*, II: 716, 715). To them "Mark Twain" was himself one of the world's greatest examples of individuality, of someone who ultimately dominated circumstances like the frontier obscurity of his birth or bankruptcy at an advanced age with a native genius that never excluded ordinary people. To them he stood for the very idea of freedom: from conventionalities, from pretense, from constraint, even, through the gift of his humor, from care.

I've said much less about his humor in this study than there is to be said, partly because it speaks best for itself, and partly because I think Twain's works serve us best in other ways, in what they reveal about the vexed history of America's continuing experiment with democracy and about the struggle we all go through to find our own selves among the many selves we enact for various audiences. But understandably, it is for his humor that many value Twain most highly, and arguably it is the best means he offers, maybe the best means that can be found, to lift the burden of the circumstances that do determine so much that is beyond our control. As he knew, humor is a response to loss and pain: "The secret source of Humor itself," he wrote, "is not joy but sorrow. There is no humor in heaven."[15] One of the best jokes he ever made not only comes out of one of the darkest periods in his life, but also in the face of the one human circumstance that may be hardest to live with. In May, 1897, a reporter for the New York *Journal* followed up a trail of rumors that Twain was on his deathbed to the author's residence in London. Twain replied to his ominous question with a note that ended by striking a terrific pose: "The report of my death was an exaggeration."[16] Eventually, of course, Samuel Clemens had to die. The report of his death sent out by a reporter from the Associated Press from Twain's last house in Connecticut on 21 April 1910 gave rise to no jokes, though probably most people did smile a bit through their sorrow when they read it, the next day, on the front page of just about every paper in the United States and in major cities around the world. That was a long time ago, but "Mark Twain," who was created out of the words Sam Clemens wrote, still has a long life ahead of him.

Appendix: "Mark Twain in His Times": An Electronic Archive

Given his enthusiasm for new inventions, Mark Twain would have loved computers and the internet – although with his knack for making bad investments, he would probably also have lost a lot of money when the dot.com bubble burst. Hank Morgan, Twain's Connecticut Yankee, would have called electronic technology a miracle, and expected it to transform the world. To me, it is a wonderful tool: there's no danger that computers will ever replace the book (itself a product of once-new technologies), but they offer a host of ways, many as yet undiscovered, to complement and enhance the relationship readers and students have with great literature. That is why since 1996, with the help of the staffs at the University of Virginia Library's Electronic Text Center and Department of Special Collections, I've been developing an online resource called "Mark Twain in His Times." I began it as a way to bring digital facsimiles of the rare materials in Virginia's Clifton Waller Barrett Collection to students in a seminar on Twain. I wanted them to learn more about Twain, but from their responses to the site I learned a lot myself, about the need to keep experimenting to find the most effective ways to use advanced technology for the study of literary texts. So "Mark Twain in His Times" is an ongoing project – one of the most inspiring and terrifying discoveries I made is that in virtual reality there is simply no place to write "The End" – but it already contains hundreds of texts and thousands of images, and has been visited by over two million users. In this appendix I'll briefly describe the site for anyone who is interested in using it to follow up this short introduction at more length.

Every primary text cited in this book is available in the site. Like the book, it is organized around Twain's six major full-length works, from *Innocents Abroad* through *Pudd'nhead Wilson*. For each of these books you can, for example, read the contemporary reviews or look at the original illustrations. Selected "PreTexts" for each Twain text help establish the relevant cultural contexts: the *Tom Sawyer* section contains excerpts from other contemporaneous children's books, for instance, and in the *Roughing It* section is a rich sampling of other depictions, in words and pictures, of the American West. Fully searchable electronic versions much of Twain's published work are also available. Searchability is one of the clearest advantages of digitizing written works: the technology can quickly tell you exactly how often, and where, Twain uses words like "decayed" or "dirty" to describe the Old World in *Innocents*, or how often, and where, he uses the word "love" throughout his writing. The hundreds of reviews, newspaper stories and obituary notices in the site are also searchable, allowing you quickly to locate what contemporary commentators had to say about "race" or "humor" or "irreverence" in Twain. In addition to the six sections on major works, the site contains sections on "Marketing Twain" (which allows you to study the subscription book system, and see how Twain's works were advertised and promoted), "Sam Clemens as Mark Twain" (which contains letters, photographs, media articles and other material enabling you to study the life of the man behind the persona), and "Mark Twain On Stage" (where you can study Twain's career as a live entertainer, from his lecture tours to his after dinner speeches, and can even, thanks to the capabilities of electronic technology, hear modern impersonators re-create Twain's famous voice).

The technology also makes it possible for users around the world to have digital access to the rare, often unique, Twain items in the Barrett Collection. The archive contains a number of his manuscripts – "A True Story," for example, was his first sustained attempt to capture an African American dialect, and by looking at the manuscript you can see how carefully he worked to get it right, at least to his eyes and ears; manuscripts of his after-dinner toasts, which he wrote out and memorized ahead of time, show how much thought and energy he devoted to these ephemeral comic performances. There is a copy of the "Memory Builder Game" that Twain first designed for his daughters, but then patented and put into commercial production – along with a new computerized "Twain memory game" that you can play and at the same time test your knowledge of his career and his times. From the Barrett Collection also come the prospectuses, or salesman's dummies, that allow us to see what prospective purchasers of *Tom Sawyer* or *Huckleberry Finn* were shown (or, in the case of the recalled *Huck Finn* prospectus, *not* shown), and a printed script that agents selling *Following the Equator* were supposed to follow, which allows us to overhear exactly what their customers were told. Such items give us much fuller access to the story of Twain's career as a popular writer.

Among the lessons I've learned from my students is that images work particularly well with electronic technology – not surprisingly, given the resemblance between a monitor screen and a TV set. Words, of course, are at the heart of Twain's achievement, but from the "lavish" illustrations of his books through his successful manufacture of his own, eventually white-suited image as a celebrity, pictures played a crucial role in his career and in establishing his meaning for his contemporaries. So the site contains a number of attempts to explore what images can reveal about the most significant issues raised by Twain's works. In the *Huck Finn* section, for instance, there is an exhibit of the various ways that Jim has been drawn in the novel's illustrated American editions 1885–1985; bringing all these different artists' re-presentations together enables users to trace how visualizations of race and slavery changed over time, and how Twain's perennially popular novel has been used to perpetuate stereotypes. Used or *ab*used – it is still up to you to decide which illustrations, if any, are true to the character of Jim as Twain's text presents him. Another exhibit, in the section called "Sam Clemens as Mark Twain," is drawn from the Barrett Collection's large grouping of Twain's letters. I say "Twain's letters," but in fact he probably never signed a letter simply as "Twain." He did, though, sign them as "Sam," as "Clemens," as "S. L. Clemens," as "Mark," as "Mark Twain," among over a dozen names he used, depending on his correspondent and his sense of himself at the moment. Looking at all these different signatures and reading the letters written over them provides a visually and, I hope, intellectually dramatic way to appreciate the complex issue of identity and selfhood in the life of Samuel Clemens and the works of Mark Twain. And of course there are a number of exhibits devoted to the way his contemporaries "saw" Twain's image, as it evolved from frontier humorist to American icon.

Modern technology has turned out to be an excellent means for taking 21st century users back in time. At least, a main goal of the site is to give readers and students many different modes of access to the late 19th and early 20th century America that Mark Twain wrote and performed for, to represent what Mark Twain and his times said about each other in ways that can speak to us today, and thus deepen our sense of what he has meant, not just as an author, but as a mythic figure in the nation's cultural consciousness. The site's internet address is: http://etext.lib.virginia.edu/railton

Notes

CHAPTER 1   GOING EAST: *INNOCENTS ABROAD*

1   *Mark Twain's Letters*, vol. 1: *1853–1866*, eds Edgar Marquess Branch, Michael B. Frank, and Kenneth M. Sanderson (Berkeley: University of California Press, 1988): 322–3.

2   *The Innocents Abroad, or The New Pilgrims' Progress* (Hartford: American Publishing Company, 1869): 27. Additional references to this text will be cited in parentheses.

3   Albert Bigelow Paine, *Mark Twain: A Biography* (New York: Harper & Brothers, 1912): 287.

4   Letter to Elisha Bliss, December 2, 1867; *Mark Twain's Letters to his Publishers*, ed. Hamlin Hill (Berkeley: University of California Press, 1967): 13.

5   Unsigned review of *Innocents Abroad* in the *Nation*, September 2, 1869.

6   This quotation and the following one are from the collection of favorable reviews that Twain and Bliss put together to help promote *Innocents Abroad*; you can find them all online in the electronic archive "Mark Twain in His Times" (see appendix).

7   Letter to Mrs Solon (Emily) Severance, October 27, 1869; *Mark Twain's Letters*, vol. 3: *1869*, eds Victor Fischer and Michael B. Frank (Berkeley: University of California Press, 1992): 374.

8   Letter to Mrs Mary Fairbanks, March 10, 1868; *Mark Twain to Mrs Fairbanks*, ed. Dixon Wecter (San Marino: Huntington Library, 1949): 24.

9   Bret Harte, review in *Overland Monthly*, January 1870.

10 Unsigned review of *Innocents Abroad* in the *National Standard*, September 2, 1869.

11 Letter to Bliss, September 3, 1869; *Mark Twain's Letters to his Publishers*: 28.

CHAPTER 2   GOING WEST: *ROUGHING IT*

1   Unsigned review of *Innocents Abroad* in the *Hartford Courant*.

2   *Innocents Abroad* (Hartford: American Publishing Company, 1869): 648. In this chapter the parenthetical references will be to *Roughing It*, ed. Harriet Elinor Smith and Edgar Marquess Branch (Berkeley: University of California Press, 1993).

3   Quoted by John McComb, editor of the San Francisco *Alta California*, in an article entitled " 'Mark Twain' Married and Settled," originally printed 14 February 1870, rpt. *Mark Twain's Letters*, Vol 4, *1870–1871*, ed. Victor Fischer and Michael B. Frank (Berkeley: University of California Press, 1995): 60–1.

4   *The Love Letters of Mark Twain*, a selection of his correspondence with Livy, was edited by Dixon Wecter (San Marino: Huntington Library, 1949). These days that source is being supplanted by the Mark Twain Papers' ongoing publication of *Mark Twain's Letters*. Twain and Livy's relationship has been recently re-considered in works like Laura E. Skandera-Trombley's *Mark Twain in the Company of Women* (Philadelphia: University of Pennsylvania, 1994) and Susan K. Harris' *Courtship of Olivia Langdon and Mark Twain* (New York: Cambridge University Press, 1996). The lines quoted in this paragraph are from a letter dated 12 January 1869; *Mark Twain's Letters*, Vol. 3, *1869*, ed. Fischer and Frank (Berkeley: University of California Press, 1988): 26.

5   Letter to "Mother & Brother & Sisters & Nephew & Niece," 5 February 1869; *Mark Twain's Letters*, 3: 85.

6   Letter to Will Bowen, 6 February 1870, *Mark Twain's Letters*, 4: 52.

7   *A Connecticut Yankee in King Arthur's Court*, ed. Bernard L. Stein (Berkeley: University of California Press, 1983): 447.

8   Albert Bigelow Paine, *Mark Twain: A Biography* (New York: Harper & Brothers, 1912): 1511.

9   In his edition of *Life on the Mississippi*, James M. Cox includes all the passages that Twain deleted, allowing you to see how he censored himself (New York: Penguin, 1984).

10 "Sandwich Islands Lecture," in *Mark Twain Speaking*, ed. Paul Fatout (Iowa City: University of Iowa Press, 1976): 6.

11 Quoted by Philip S. Foner, *Mark Twain: Social Critic* (New York: International Publishers, 1958): 239.

12 *Following the Equator* (Hartford: American Publishing Company, 1897): 213.

13 "To the Person Sitting in Darkness" (1901; rpt. *Mark Twain: Collected Tales, Sketches, Speeches, & Essays*, 2 vols, ed. Louis J. Budd (New York: Library of America, 1992): II, 465.

14 "The Significance of the Frontier in American History" (1893; rpt. *Rereading Frederick Jackson Turner*, ed. John Mack Faragher (New York: Henry Holt, 1994): 31, 32.

15 William Dean Howells, unsigned review of *Roughing It*, in *The Atlantic* 29 (June 1872): 754.

CHAPTER 3 GOING HOME: *Tom Sawyer*

1 *The Adventures of Tom Sawyer*, ed. John C. Gerber and Paul Baender (Berkeley: University of California Press, 1982): 54; additional references to this work will be cited in parentheses.

2 Howells' letter to his father (1875), quoted in *Mark Twain: A Biography*, by Albert Bigelow Paine (New York: Harper & Brothers, 1912): 572–3.

3 Letter to Howells, 5 July 1875; in *Selected Mark Twain-Howells Letters*, ed. Anderson, Gibson and Smith (New York: Atheneum, 1968): 49. In this letter, in fact, Twain is writing to say that, although he would "dearly like to see [*Tom Sawyer*] in the Atlantic [magazine]," he needs more money than the magazine could pay.

4 William Dean Howells, review of *Tom Sawyer* in the *Atlantic* 37 (May 1876).

5 In 1873 Bliss's company published, as the first novel ever sold by subscription, *The Gilded Age: A Tale of Today*, which Twain co-authored with Hartford neighbor Charles Dudley Warner; technically this satirical account of politics and other contemporary corruptions is the "first novel by Mark Twain," but *Tom Sawyer* is the first full-length work of fiction he wrote by himself.

6 *Mark Twain's Letters*, ed. Albert Bigelow Paine (New York: Harper & Brothers, 1917): 477.

7 Letter to Howells, 5 July 1875; *Selected Twain-Howells Letters*: 48.

8 Letter to William Bowen, 6 February 1870, *Mark Twain's Letters*, vol. 4: *1870–1871*, ed. Victor Fischer and Michael B. Frank (Berkeley: University of California Press, 1995): 50–2.

9 Jane Addams, *Twenty Years at Hull-House* (1910; rpt. New York: Signet Classic, 1961): 81.

10 *Life on the Mississippi*, ed. James M. Cox (New York: Penguin Books, 1984): 64. The passage originally appeared in the first installment of "Old Times on the Mississippi," published in the January, 1875, issue of *The Atlantic Monthly*. The "Old Times" sequence has been reprinted in several different anthologies of Twain's work, but still the most convenient way to read the sketches is in *Life on Mississippi*, where they comprise chapters 4–17.

11 Hamilton W. Mabie, "Mark Twain the Humorist," in *The Outlook* 87 (23 November 1907): 650–1.

CHAPTER 4   RUNNING AWAY: *Adventures of Huckleberry Finn*

1 Ernest Hemingway, *The Green Hills of Africa* (New York: Charles Scribner's Sons, 1935): 22.
2 Note the difference within the similarity of their names: there is no "The" in *Huck Finn's* title
3 The word "outcast" is used twice to describe Huck in the scene that introduces him into *The Adventures of Tom Sawyer* (Berkeley: University of California Press, 1982): 48–9.
4 *Adventures of Huckleberry Finn*, ed. Victor Fischer and Lin Salamo (Berkeley: University of California Press, 2001): 24; subsequent references to the novel will be made in parentheses.
5 Gale has published the second half of the manuscript in a facsimile edition (Detroit: Gale Research Co., 1983). The first half of the manuscript, long assumed to be permanently lost, was discovered in an attic in Los Angeles in 1990; the full manuscript is now available in the *CD-ROM Edition* of *Huck Finn*, edited by Victor A. Doyno (Buffalo and Erie County Library Foundation Board, 2003).
6 *Tom Sawyer*: 10.
7 *Tom Sawyer*: 3.
8 In a notebook entry about *Huck Finn* Twain remembers how, during his own childhood in Hannibal, "the whole community was agreed as to one thing – the awful sacredness of slave property"; helping "a hunted slave" was "a much baser crime" than stealing a horse or a cow (quoted by Walter Blair, *Mark Twain and "Huck Finn"* [Berkeley: University of California Press, 1960]: 144).
9 Quoted by Henry Nash Smith, "Introduction," *Adventures of Huckleberry Finn* (Boston: Houghton Mifflin Company, 1958): xvi.
10 In addition to the Introduction cited in the previous note, see Smith's *Mark Twain: The Development of a Writer* (1962; rpt. New York: Atheneum, 1972): 113–37.
11 *Innocents Abroad* (Hartford: American Publishing Company, 1869): 486.
12 John Wallace, "The Case Against Huck Finn," in *Satire or Evasion? Black Perspectives on Huckleberry Finn*, ed. Leonard, Tenney and Davis (Durham: Duke University Press, 1992): 16. Wallace has been the spokesperson for a number of campaigns, some successful, to ban *Huck Finn* from school systems.

13 Quoted by Shelley Fisher Fishkin, *Lighting Out for the Territory: Reflections on Mark Twain and American Culture* (New York: Oxford University Press, 1996): 100. Taylor was an actor playing Jim in a dramatization of the novel at the time.
14 For a summary of this interpretation, see Fishkin, *Was Huck Black? Mark Twain and African American Voices* (New York: Oxford University Press, 1993): 68–76.
15 Letter to Cha[rle]s Webster, 14 April 1884; *Mark Twain Letter's to His Publishers*, ed. Hamlin Hill (Berkeley: University of California Press, 1967): 249.
16 Letter to Livy Clemens, 29 December 1884; *The Love Letters of Mark Twain*, ed. Dixon Wecter (New York: Harper & Brothers, 1949): 223–4.
17 Letters to Livy, from Pittsburg, 29 December 1884, and from Chicago, 17 January 1885; *Love Letters*: 223 and 230–1.
18 *The* (Cincinnati) *Enquirer*, 4 January 1885; *The* (Indianapolis) *Journal*, 8 February 1885.
19 "Introduction," *Adventures of Huckleberry Finn*, ed. Walter Blair and Victor Fischer (Berkeley: University of California Press, 1988): xlvii.
20 The hardcover University of California edition of *Huck Finn* cited in the previous note includes ads and other promotional material in its appendices.
21 Letter to Webster, 24 May 1884; in *Mark Twain Businessman*, ed. Samuel C. Webster (Boston: Little, Brown, 1946): 255.
22 Letter to Webster, 11 June 1884; in *Mark Twain Businessman*: 260.
23 In "Illustrating *Huckleberry Finn*," written almost half a century later, Kemble talks about the way the "negro drawings" he did for Twain's novel launched his career as a specialist in representing African Americans (*The Colophon* [February 1930]: 1–8).

CHAPTER 5   LOST IN TIME: *A Connecticut Yankee in King Arthur's Court*

1 *Innocents Abroad* (Hartford: American Publishing Company, 1869): 511.
2 Mark Twain, *The Mysterious Stranger*, ed. William H. Gibson (Berkeley: University of California Press, 1970): 404.
3 *Mark Twain's Notebooks and Journals*, 3 vols., ed. Frederick Anderson et al. (Berkeley: University of California Press, 1979) 3: 78.
4 *The Autobiography of Mark Twain*, arranged and ed. by Charles Neider (New York: Harper Perennial, 1990): 273.
5 *The Mysterious Stranger*, pp. 165–6.
6 Twain, *Life on the Mississippi*, ed. James M. Cox (New York: Penguin Books, 1984): 327.

7   Twain, *A Connecticut Yankee in King Arthur's Court*, ed. Bernard L. Stein (Berkeley: University of California Press, 1983): 112. Additional references to this paperback edition of the novel will be made in parentheses in the text.

8   Edward Bellamy's *Looking Backward: 2000–1887*, about traveling into the future, came out in 1888, a year before Twain's novel, but Twain began writing *Connecticut Yankee* two years before Bellamy's book appeared.

9   This and the other publicity items discussed in this paragaph are included as appendices to the University of California hardcover edition of *Connecticut Yankee*, ed. Stein (Berkeley: 1979): 523–41.

10 The reviews in this paragraph are available in *Mark Twain: The Critical Heritage*, ed. Frederick Anderson (London: Routledge & Kegan Paul, 1971): 148–76 – *Harper's Magazine* (January 1890): 319; *Herald* (15 December 1889): 17; *Plumas National* (5 July 1890): 2; *Literary World* (15 February 1890): 173.

11 Twain's *Century* commentaries are also published as an appendix to the University of California hardcover *Yankee*: 542–3.

12 Kaplan's chapter on this connection is called "The Yankee and the Machine" – *Mr. Clemens and Mark Twain* (New York: Simon and Schuster, 1966): 280–311.

13 Letter to Mary Fairbanks, 16 November 1886; *Mark Twain to Mrs. Fairbanks*, ed. Dixon Wecter (San Marino: Huntington Library, 1949): 258.

14 Quoted in Kaplan, p. 281.

15 Letter to William Dean Howells, 21 October 1889; *Selected Mark Twain-Howells Letters*, ed. Anderson, Gibson and Smith (New York: Atheneum, 1968): 288.

16 Letter to Olivia Clemens, 4 February 1885; *The Love Letters of Mark Twain*, ed. Dixon Wecter (New York: Harper & Brothers, 1949): 229–30.

CHAPTER 6   LOOKING FOR REFUGE:
Pudd'nhead Wilson & "HADLEYBURG"

1   Albert Bigelow Paine, *Mark Twain: A Biography* (New York: Harper & Brothers, 1912): 1575.

2   Quoted in Justin Kaplan, *Mr. Clemens and Mark Twain* (New York: Simon and Schuster, 1966): 341.

3   Long after Twain's death, scholars began publishing these fragments; there is a well-chosen sampling of them in *The Devil's Race-Track: Mark Twain's Great Dark Writings*, ed. John S. Tuckey (Berkeley: University of California Press, 1966).

4 *Mark Twain's Wound*, ed. Lewis Leary (New York: Crowell, 1962), presents both sides in the debate that raged through the 1920s and 1930s, and in many ways still organizes the critical discussion of the meaning of Twain's work and life.

5 *The Tragedy of Pudd'nhead Wilson and the Comedy of Those Extraordinary Twins*, published as *Pudd'nhead Wilson*, ed. Malcolm Bradbury (New York: Penguin Putnam, 1969): 230. Subsequent references to this text will be in parentheses.

6 Anonymous article, "The Tocci Twins," in *Scientific American* (December 1891); this may have been where Twain saw their picture.

7 Freud himself was a "delighted" member of the audience at Twain's first lecture in Vienna (1 February 1898) and knew Twain's work well, referring to it a number of times in his own writing (cf. Carl Dolmetsch, *"Our Famous Guest": Mark Twain in Vienna* [Athens: University of Georgia Press, 1992]: 266ff.).

8 *The Prince and the Pauper*, ed. Victor Fischer and Michael B. Frank (Berkeley: University of California, 1983): 296.

9 The usefulness of fingerprints as "identifiers" was discovered by an Englishman named Francis Galton, whose 1892 book on the subject was Twain's source for using fingerprints in the novel. Galton, who later coined the term "eugenics," explains that his original "great expectation" was that patterns in fingerprints would reveal "racial differences"; he admits, however, that he could not find any correlation between race and fingerprints (Galton, *Finger Prints* [London: Macmillan and Co., 1892]).

10 Anonymous review of *Pudd'nhead Wilson* in *The Hartford Times*, 18 February 1895.

11 The drawing is by E. W. Kemble, the same artist whom Twain hired to illustrate *Huck Finn*. As Werner Sollors has recently shown, Kemble's representation of Roxy is actually the woman whose head is just visible behind the man's right shoulder, and who does look more like the novel's description of Roxy than the "aunt" figure at the center. This identification would have been clearer to purchasers of the American Publishing Company's "Édition de Luxe" of *Pudd'nhead Wilson*, also published in 1899. They would have seen Kemble's other representation of Roxy, showing her "among the Field Hands," and might have looked back at "Roxy Harvesting among the Kitchens" to spot her in the background. But this "édition" was limited to 1,000 numbered copies, while the Harpers' version, with no second illustration, sold hundreds of thousands of copies over the years. It seems unlikely that many of its readers even noticed this second female figure. (See Sollors, "Was Roxy Black?" in *Mixed Race Literature*, ed. Jonathan Brennan [Stanford: Stanford University Press, 2002]: 70–87.)

12 Paul B. Barringer, *The American Negro: His Past and Future* (Raleigh: Edwards and Broughton, 1900).

13 "The Man That Corrupted Hadleyburg," in *Mark Twain: Collected Tales, Sketches, Speeches & Essays*, 2 vols., ed. Louis J. Budd (New York: Library of America, 1992): II, 417. The story was originally published in *Harper's Monthly* magazine, December 1899; subsequent references to it will be to the Library of America text, cited in parentheses as *"Tales,"* followed by the volume and page number.

14 *The Mysterious Stranger*, ed. William M. Gibson (Berkeley: University of California Press, 1969): 166.

15 *Following the Equator* (Hartford: American Publishing Company, 1897): 119.

16 "The report of my death was an exaggeration" is among Twain's best-known one-liners, though it is often quoted inaccurately. You can see an image of his original 1897 hand-written note at Barbara Schmidt's website "Mark Twain Quotations, Newspaper Collections, & Related Resources" (http://www.twainquotes.com).

Index

Clemens' life and Twain's works and themes are indexed under the entry "Mark Twain." The entries for "*Life*" under "Mark Twain" are listed chronologically.